How to restore

Honda
Fours

Covers CB350, 400, 500, 550, 650 & 750
SOHC Fours 1969-1982

YOUR step-by-step colour illustrated guide
to complete restoration

Ricky Burns

Also from Veloce Publishing –

Enthusiast's Restoration Manual Series
Beginner's Guide to Classic Motorcycle Restoration YOUR step-by-step guide to setting up a workshop, choosing a project, dismantling, sourcing parts, renovating & rebuilding classic motorcycles from the 1970s & 1980s, The (Burns)
Citroën 2CV, How to Restore (Porter)
Classic Large Frame Vespa Scooters, How to Restore (Paxton)
Classic Car Bodywork, How to Restore (Thaddeus)
Classic British Car Electrical Systems (Astley)
Classic Car Electrics (Thaddeus)
Classic Cars, How to Paint (Thaddeus)
Ducati Bevel Twins 1971 to 1986 (Falloon)
How to restore Honda Fours – YOUR step-by-step colour illustrated guide to complete restoration (Burns)
Jaguar E-type (Crespin)
Reliant Regal, How to Restore (Payne)
Triumph TR2, 3, 3A, 4 & 4A, How to Restore (Williams)
Triumph TR5/250 & 6, How to Restore (Williams)
Triumph TR7/8, How to Restore (Williams)
Volkswagen Beetle, How to Restore (Tyler)
VW Bay Window Bus (Paxton)
Yamaha FS1-E, How to Restore (Watts)

Essential Buyer's Guide Series
Alfa Romeo Alfasud (Metcalfe)
Alfa Romeo Alfetta: all saloon/sedan models 1972 to 1984 & coupé models 1974 to 1987 (Metcalfe)
Alfa Romeo Giulia GT Coupé (Booker)
Alfa Romeo Giulia Spider (Booker)
Audi TT (Davies)
Audi TT Mk2 2006 to 2014 (Durnan)
Austin-Healey Big Healeys (Trummel)
BMW Boxer Twins (Henshaw)
BMW E30 3 Series 1981 to 1994 (Hosier)
BMW GS (Henshaw)
BMW X5 (Saunders)
BMW Z3 Roadster (Fishwick)
BMW Z4: E85 Roadster and E86 Coupé including M and Alpina 2003 to 2009 (Smitheram)
BSA 350, 441 & 500 Singles (Henshaw)
BSA 500 & 650 Twins (Henshaw)
BSA Bantam (Henshaw)
Choosing, Using & Maintaining Your Electric Bicycle (Henshaw)
Citroën 2CV (Paxton)
Citroën DS & ID (Heilig)
Cobra Replicas (Ayre)
Corvette C2 Sting Ray 1963-1967 (Falconer)
Datsun 240Z 1969 to 1973 (Newlyn)
DeLorean DMC-12 1981 to 1983 (Williams)
Ducati Bevel Twins (Falloon)
Ducati Desmodue Twins (Falloon)
Ducati Desmoquattro Twins – 851, 888, 916, 996, 998, ST4 1988 to 2004 (Falloon)
Fiat 500 & 600 (Bobbitt)
Ford Capri (Paxton)
Ford Escort Mk1 & Mk2 (Williamson)
Ford Focus RS/ST 1st Generation (Williamson)
Ford Model A – All Models 1927 to 1931 (Buckley)
Ford Model T – All models 1909 to 1927 (Barker)
Ford Mustang – First Generation 1964 to 1973 (Cook)
Ford Mustang – Fifth Generation (2005-2014) (Cook)
Ford RS Cosworth Sierra & Escort (Williamson)
Harley-Davidson Big Twins (Henshaw)
Hillman Imp (Morgan)
Hinckley Triumph triples & fours 750, 900, 955, 1000, 1050, 1200 – 1991-2009 (Henshaw)
Honda CBR FireBlade (Henshaw)
Honda CBR600 Hurricane (Henshaw)
Honda SOHC Fours 1969-1984 (Henshaw)
Jaguar E-Type 3.8 & 4.2 litre (Crespin)
Jaguar E-type V12 5.3 litre (Crespin)
Jaguar Mark 1 & 2 (All models including Daimler 2.5-litre V8) 1955 to 1969 (Thorley)
Jaguar New XK 2005-2014 (Thorley)
Jaguar S-Type – 1999 to 2007 (Thorley)
Jaguar X-Type – 2001 to 2009 (Thorley)
Jaguar XJ-S (Crespin)
Jaguar XJ6, XJ8 & XJR (Thorley)
Jaguar XK 120, 140 & 150 (Thorley)
Jaguar XK8 & XKR (1996-2005) (Thorley)
Jaguar/Daimler XJ 1994-2003 (Crespin)
Jaguar/Daimler XJ40 (Crespin)
Jaguar/Daimler XJ6, XJ12 & Sovereign (Crespin)
Kawasaki Z1 & Z900 (Orritt)
Land Rover Discovery Series 1 (1989-1998) (Taylor)
Land Rover Discovery Series 2 (1998-2004) (Taylor)
Land Rover Series I, II & IIA (Thurman)
Land Rover Series III (Thurman)
Lotus Elan, S1 to Sprint and Plus 2 to Plus 2S 130/5 1962 to 1974 (Vale)
Lotus Europa, S1, S2, Twin-cam & Special 1966 to 1975 (Vale)
Lotus Seven replicas & Caterham 7: 1973-2013 (Hawkins)
Mazda MX-5 Miata (Mk1 1989-97 & Mk2 98-2001) (Crook)
Mazda RX-8 (Parish)
Mercedes-Benz 190: all 190 models (W201 series) 1982 to 1993 (Parish)
Mercedes-Benz 280-560SL & SLC (Bass)
Mercedes-Benz G-Wagen (Greene)
Mercedes-Benz Pagoda 230SL, 250SL & 280SL roadsters & coupés (Bass)
Mercedes-Benz S-Class W126 Series (Zoporowski)
Mercedes-Benz S-Class Second Generation W116 Series (Parish)
Mercedes-Benz SL R129-series 1989 to 2001 (Parish)
Mercedes-Benz SLK (Bass)
Mercedes-Benz W123 (Parish)
Mercedes-Benz W124 – All models 1984-1997 (Zoporowski)
MG Midget & A-H Sprite (Horler)
MG TD, TF & TF1500 (Jones)
MGA 1955-1962 (Crosier)
MGB & MGB GT (Williams)
MGF & MG TF (Hawkins)
Mini (Paxton)
Morgan Plus 4 (Benfield)
Morris Minor & 1000 (Newell)
Moto Guzzi 2-valve big twins (Falloon)
New Mini (Collins)
Norton Commando (Henshaw)
Peugeot 205 GTI (Blackburn)
Piaggio Scooters – all modern two-stroke & four-stroke automatic models 1991 to 2016 (Willis)
Porsche 356 (Johnson)
Porsche 911 (964) (Streather)
Porsche 911 (991) (Streather)
Porsche 911 (993) (Streather)
Porsche 911 (996) (Streather)
Porsche 911 (997) – Model years 2004 to 2009 (Streather)
Porsche 911 (997) – Second generation models 2009 to 2012 (Streather)
Porsche 911 Carrera 3.2 (Streather)
Porsche 911SC (Streather)
Porsche 924 – All models 1976 to 1988 (Hodgkins)
Porsche 928 (Hemmings)
Porsche 930 Turbo & 911 (930) Turbo (Streather)
Porsche 944 (Higgins)
Porsche 981 Boxster & Cayman (Streather)
Porsche 986 Boxster (Streather)
Porsche 987 Boxster and Cayman 1st generation (2005-2009) (Streather)
Porsche 987 Boxster and Cayman 2nd generation (2009-2012) (Streather)
Range Rover – First Generation models 1970 to 1996 (Taylor)
Range Rover – Second Generation 1994-2001 (Taylor)
Range Rover – Third Generation L322 (2002-2012) (Taylor)
Reliant Scimitar GTE (Payne)
Rolls-Royce Silver Shadow & Bentley T-Series (Bobbitt)
Rover 2000, 2200 & 3500 (Marrocco)
Royal Enfield Bullet (Henshaw)
Subaru Impreza (Hobbs)
Sunbeam Alpine (Barker)
Triumph 350 & 500 Twins (Henshaw)
Triumph Bonneville (Henshaw)
Triumph Herald & Vitesse (Ayre)
Triumph Spitfire and GT6 (Ayre)
Triumph Stag (Mort)
Triumph Thunderbird, Trophy & Tiger (Henshaw)
Triumph TR2 & TR3 - All models (including 3A & 3B) 1953 to 1962 (Conners)
Triumph TR4/4A & TR5/250 - All models 1961 to 1968 (Child & Battyll)
Triumph TR6 (Williams)
Triumph TR7 & TR8 (Williams)
Triumph Trident & BSA Rocket III (Rooke)
TVR Chimaera and Griffith (Kitchen)
TVR S-series (Kitchen)
Velocette 350 & 500 Singles 1946 to 1970 (Henshaw)
Vespa Scooters – Classic 2-stroke models 1960-2008 (Paxton)
Volkswagen Bus (Copping)
Volkswagen Transporter T4 (1990-2003) (Copping/Cservenka)
VW Golf GTI (Copping)
VW Beetle (Copping)
Volvo 700/900 Series (Beavis)
Volvo P1800/1800S, E & ES 1961 to 1973 (Murray)

General Motorcycle Books
BMW Cafe Racers (Cloesen)
BMW Custom Motorcycles – Choppers, Cruisers, Bobbers, Trikes & Quads (Cloesen)
Bonjour – Is this Italy? (Turner)
British 250cc Racing Motorcycles (Pereira)
BSA Bantam Bible, The (Henshaw)
BSA Motorcycles – the final evolution (Jones)
Ducati 750 Bible, The (Falloon)
Ducati 750 SS 'round-case' 1974, The Book of the (Falloon)
Ducati 860, 900 and Mille Bible, The (Falloon)
Ducati Monster Bible, The (Falloon)
Fine Art of the Motorcycle Engine, The (Peirce)
From Crystal Palace to Red Square – A Hapless Biker's Road to Russia (Turner)
Funky Mopeds (Skelton)
Italian Cafe Racers (Cloesen)
Italian Custom Motorcycles (Cloesen)
Kawasaki Triples Bible, The (Walker)
Lambretta Bible, The (Davies)
Laverda Twins & Triples Bible 1968-1986 (Falloon)
Moto Guzzi Sport & Le Mans Bible, The (Falloon)
Motorcycle Apprentice (Cakebread)
Motorcycle GP Racing in the 1960s (Pereira)
Motorcycle Road & Racing Chassis Designs (Noakes)
MV Agusta Fours, The book of the classic (Falloon)
Scooters & Microcars, The A-Z of Popular (Dan)
Scooter Lifestyle (Grainger)
SCOOTER MANIA! – Recollections of the Isle of Man International Scooter Rally (Jackson)
Triumph Bonneville Bible (59-83) (Henshaw)
Triumph Bonneville!, Save the – The inside story of the Meriden Workers' Co-op (Rosamond)
Triumph Motorcycles & the Meriden Factory (Hancox)
Triumph Speed Twin & Thunderbird Bible (Woolridge)
Triumph Tiger Cub Bible (Estall)
Triumph Trophy Bible (Woolridge)
TT Talking The TT's most exciting era – As seen by Manx Radio TT's lead commentator 2004-2012 (Lambert)
Velocette Motorcycles – MSS to Thruxton – New Third Edition (Burris)

www.veloce.co.uk

First published in September 2014, reprinted August 2020 by Veloce Publishing Limited, Veloce House, Parkway Farm Business Park, Middle Farm Way, Poundbury, Dorchester DT1 3AR, England. Tel 01305 260068 / Fax 01305 250479 / e-mail info@veloce.co.uk / web www.veloce.co.uk or www.velocebooks.com.
ISBN: 978-1-845847-46-3 UPC: 6-36847-04746-7
© Ricky Burns and Veloce Publishing 2014 & 2020. All rights reserved. With the exception of quoting brief passages for the purpose of review, no part of this publication may be recorded, reproduced or transmitted by any means, including photocopying, without the written permission of Veloce Publishing Ltd. Throughout this book logos, model names and designations, etc, have been used for the purposes of identification, illustration and decoration. Such names are the property of the trademark holder as this is not an official publication. Readers with ideas for automotive books, or books on other transport or related hobby subjects, are invited to write to the editorial director of Veloce Publishing at the above address. British Library Cataloguing in Publication Data – A catalogue record for this book is available from the British Library. Typesetting, design and page make-up all by Veloce Publishing Ltd on Apple Mac. Printed and bound by CPI Group (UK) Ltd, Croydon, CR0 4YY.

How to restore

Honda Fours

Covers CB350, 400, 500, 550, 650 & 750
SOHC Fours 1969-1982

YOUR step-by-step colour illustrated guide
to complete restoration

Ricky Burns

VELOCE PUBLISHING
THE PUBLISHER OF FINE AUTOMOTIVE BOOKS

Contents

Introduction 6

Chapter 1 – Project assessment . . 7
First impressions. 8
Basic engine assessment 9
If the engine does not start 9
The fuel tank and seat 9
   Checking the fuel tank 9
   Checking the seat 10
Frame and forks 10

Chapter 2 – Sourcing parts 12
The internet 12
Clubs and forums 12
Magazines 13
The auto jumble 13

Chapter 3 – Getting started 15
Starting the strip down 16
   Removing the seat and tank . . 17
   Removing the engine 18

Chapter 4 – Cleaning & polishing . . 29
De-greasing 29
Ultrasonic cleaning 30
Equipment 31
Metal polishing wheels and
compounds 31

Polishing mops 31
Polishing compounds 32
Chrome polishing 32
Rust removal 33
   DIY chrome plating 35

Chapter 5 – The engine 36
Engine unit 37
   What you will need 37
   Engine out 38
   Cylinder head and barrels 41
   The bottom end 49
Rebuilding the engine 55

**Chapter 6 – Brakes, wheels &
tyres** 71
Hydraulic disk brakes 71
   Rebuilding the brake calliper . . . 72
   Re-building the master cylinder . . 76
Drum brakes 78
   Cables 78
   Oiling cables 80
Wheels 80
Tyres 83

**Chapter 7 – Fuel & exhaust
systems** 86
The fuel tank 86
   Fuel tap 87

The carburettor 90
The exhaust system 98

Chapter 8 – Electrics 100
Faults and precautions 100
The battery 101
Wiring diagrams 101
Ignition and charging systems . . . 103
The charging and starting
   systems 105

**Chapter 9 – Spraying, decals &
badges** 108
Tools and materials needed 109
   Preparation 109
   Priming 109
   Finish coat 109
Stripping paint 109
Fitting the decals 112
   The main rules 112
   Badges 116

Chapter 10 – Clocks & switches . 118
Rebuilding the switch gear 121
Clocks and gauges 123

Chapter 11 – The seat 128

Chapter 12 – The forks. 138

Chapter 13 – Rebuild. 144
Frame build and rear end 144
Rebuilding the front end 148
Fitting the rear wheel 153
Refitting the engine 156
Fitting the exhaust 161

Chapter 14 – Final details 164
Cables 164

Brake lights 165
Throttle cable 165
Mirrors 166
Tyre pressure and tread 166
Split pins 166
Lights. 166
First start up 166
The first ride 167

Chapter 15 – Safe riding 168
The country road story 168
Overtaking 169

Bad road conditions 169
Training. 170

Index. 175

Introduction

During the late sixties and early seventies, the motorcycle world experienced a period of rapid change, well-established motorcycle manufacturers apparently ignoring the steady progress with which Japanese manufacturers were making inroads into their traditional markets, content to continue with old, out of date models ... with devastating results. In the ensuing technological race, the four main Japanese motorcycle manufacturers – Honda, Suzuki, Kawasaki and Yamaha – leapt ahead of the rest of the world in terms of innovation and production.

The British motorcycle industry had sat on its laurels for years, relying on reputation and engineering superiority from previous decades to see it into the future. Now, Japanese motorcycle manufacturers were busy copying and improving on the designs and manufacturing practices it traditionally employed.

As a schoolboy, I remember watching a news story comparing a modern Japanese motorcycle with the equivalent British bike. The British motorcycle had no electric start, used old drum brakes, leaked oil and was more expensive to purchase than the new Honda, which had many modern advantages such as an electric start. It was also oil-tight, super-reliable.

The British motorcycle industry was slow to react to the progress made by the Japanese Big Four in general, and Honda in particular, and this marked the beginning of the end of the biggest motorcycle industry in the world at that time.

The Japanese manufacturers often built motorcycles in ranges. Suzuki had the 2-stroke triples, as did Kawasaki. Honda liked to stay with 4-stroke engines – four cylinders and twins in particular – and Yamaha had its racy 2-stroke twins. There was little difference between some of the motorcycles in these groups other than engine capacity.

This book covers one such range, the Honda SOHC Fours. Given that these motorcycles sold in vast numbers, this book will appeal to a wide audience, who, like me, loved that era of motorcycle history.

How to Restore Your Honda Four covers the single overhead cam models from 1969-1982 (some being registered even later). It was decided early on to use a CB750 as the basis for this book. due to the vast number sold, and because it had the longest-running SOHC production run, and a CB350 Four because its engine is similar to the other small models in the range, However, the restoration techniques apply to all Honda SOHC models, whatever the engine size.

From choosing your project through complete strip down and rebuild, right up to the first start up and ride, this step-by-step guide covers a relatively wide range of models, so should be used in conjunction with the appropriate workshop manual and handbook for your motorcycle.

Enjoy and good luck with your restoration.

Ricky Burns

Chapter 1
Project assessment

Whether you already have your bike or are about to buy one, it's always a good idea to set out a rebuild plan. To do this you will need to carry out a project assessment, which, once done, will provide you with a better understanding of the work and cost involved in your restoration.

For a moment, though, let us imagine the following scenario. A keen motorcyclist has decided to give up motorcycling due to advancing years. He (or she) has a low mileage, early Honda CB750 (or any other engine size, for that matter) that they have loved dearly for years, always taking great care of it, and maintaining it regardless of cost. Now, the bike is stored in a dry garage under a protective covering. You hear about this bike and, after a visit to see it, you part with some hard-earned cash to buy it. You get it home, charge the battery, fill it with fresh fuel, and – hey presto! – after a few attempts it starts and runs like a dream: no oil leaks, and everything electrical works just fine.

A dream scenario, I know, but it could happen, and occasionally does. I have been lucky in the past and you may be lucky in the future. Bikes like that are out there, still: some put away

1.0 This is why we do it. Left for over twenty years, and almost broken for spares, this beautiful little Honda CB350 Four was saved and lovingly restored by the author. Although the original exhaust pipes had long ago rusted away, four silencers were found and adapted to retain the 4-into-4 look.

nicely. More usually, though, matters are not quite as straightforward.

Let's look at the more common scenario. The bike you are about to buy – some twenty years after it was last used – had an owner who didn't service it well, as a result of which it developed a mechanical problem. Not a classic bike then, its owner put it to one side and purchased a newer

HOW TO RESTORE HONDA FOURS

machine. It was not economically viable for him to spend money on the old Honda and so it gradually fell into a state of neglect. The owner's friend needed a few parts for his Honda, and takes these from YOUR Honda! The old Honda is left, forgotten: inside, with a bit of luck but more likely outside, under a covering of sorts.

You are enthusiastic about fixing up this old Honda; getting it looking just like new and hearing the engine run like a sewing machine again, just like it used to. If you can achieve this – and you certainly can – your feeling of satisfaction will be huge, and your newly-restored Honda could be with you for years; even becoming part of a collection if you go on to restore more motorcycles in the future.

So, what will you be up against? For a start, it's likely that the engine will be seized after being motionless for so long, and this can sometimes be remedied – with patience – over a few weeks, although could be an engine-out job, and at least a partial rebuild. You already know that parts are missing, and these may be hard to come by now. The paintwork will have rusted, as would the chrome plating. Left standing, parts begin to seize and rubbers begin to crack; the chrome and alloy oxidise. And you will need to identify the original mechanical problem and fix this during your restoration. Now, for us enthusiasts this is all part of the fun ... isn't it? Well, for me it is.

Many of the faults listed below are common on most projects, so don't be too worried if your bike has some of these defects: after all, this is a restoration project. If you know what to look for it will help you decide if this is the right project for you – and be a useful bargaining tool when negotiating a price with the seller.

The following are things to look out for, so make up a checklist for when you first view your project. All problems can be overcome, but the worse the problem, the more expensive it will be to rectify.

FIRST IMPRESSIONS
What is your overall first impression of the motorcycle. Is it all there? Are there obviously parts missing? Side covers, indicator lenses, levers and lights are common missing parts.

Does the owner have the keys? If not, it will be necessary to buy a complete set of locks, if it's not possible to have original keys made.

Are the usual documents and paperwork available? Having these will save time when putting the bike on the road.

Does the owner have any old workshop manuals? Many owners do, and it's a real bonus if these are included in the sale.

Are there any spare parts? Again many owners have a box full of bits that they consider worthless, so take them if they are available as you will often find a part that you need later on.

Does it look as though the bike just stopped being used and was left as it was the last time it was ridden, or does it seem that someone has tinkered with it? Tell-tale signs in this respect are screws not replaced; side panels and battery missing.

1.1 An engine mounting bolt with a nut missing: it didn't say that in the advert!

1.2 Incorrect bolts have been fitted to make the bike look complete.

1.3 The wiring loom here has been cut right through.

PROJECT ASSESSMENT

BASIC ENGINE ASSESSMENT
Let's begin with a basic engine check. Before attempting to start an engine, ensure it has sufficient oil. If it starts and runs, great. Look for excessive smoke: on first start-up the mixture will be rich with the choke on, and the exhaust may look a little smoky until the engine is warmed up. Don't confuse smoke (darker with a more oily smell) with steam, however. Moisture can build up in the exhaust of a bike that's not been used for some time, and turns to steam when it's first started, but this will burn off after a little while.

Are there any unusual noises? Listen for internal knocking or rattles. Honda Four engines are a little noisy, particularly if tickover speed is set too low, but they should quieten once warmed up.

You can usually hear cam chain noise, but it may simply be a matter of re-setting the tensioner to adjust this. If you are unfamiliar with how an engine should sound, take along a friend who has more experience in such matters

1.4 Almost all of the rocker cover bolts were missing on this engine.

If the engine does not start
Does the engine turn over (you may have to use the kickstart as there is unlikely to be any life in the battery)? This will indicate whether the engine is seized, in which case, it could be expensive to resolve, but not always.

Does the engine have all its sparkplugs? It's not a good sign – especially if the bike has been stored outside – for a sparkplug to be missing, as moisture could have got in and caused cylinder damage. I had to buy a complete cylinder head for a Honda CB350/4 because water had corroded the head behind a valve seat – and all because a sparkplug had been left out.

Is it possible to pull in the clutch lever and open the throttle smoothly? It takes a long time for these controls to seize, so their condition will give you an idea of how long the bike has been standing.

Can you select all of the gears? Try rocking the bike backward and forward whilst moving the gearlever through the gears (you may need help with this if the bike is heavy).

THE FUEL TANK AND SEAT
Checking the fuel tank
It might be difficult to find a secondhand fuel tank, and any that are available will command a high asking price. I have seen new old stock fuel tanks for sale but aftermarket fuel tanks are not normally available.

Take a good look at the tank: cosmetic problems can be rectified; it is holes that we're really looking for. Take off the fuel cap and have a good look inside the tank. Is it clean or dirty, and, if the latter, how bad is it? A replacement tank is likely to be required if there are sizeable holes, although smaller holes can be repaired.

Does the tank retain its shape, without bad dents and/or damage? Although this can be overcome, as with everything else, the worse the problem is, the more expensive it will be to rectify.

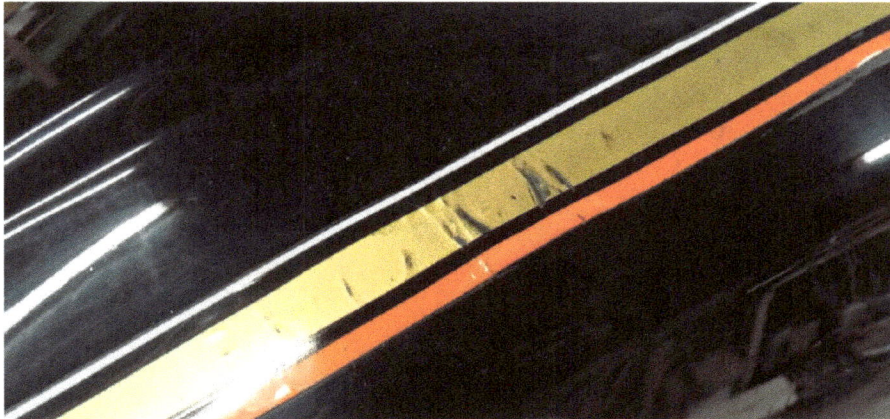

1.5 Is the tank rust-free inside and out? This example is in quite good condition, with only the stripe and paintwork requiring attention.

1.6 This tank has rusted through completely, leaving a large hole.

HOW TO RESTORE HONDA FOURS

Checking the seat

It is not usual to find a seat cover still intact. New covers are available so a torn example is not a big problem, but make sure that the frame and seat base are in good condition. Check that all of the seat rubbers are still in place: usually, some are missing, but new ones are available.

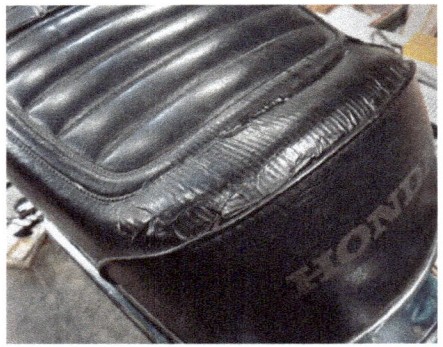

1.7 Unfortunately, this seat will need recovering because it has a tear under the black tape.

All seats had metal bases that will rust. A little rust can be dealt with but a badly rotted base will require replacement – if you can find one. If the seat base is rotten, it's likely the hinges will be loose, causing a problem with securing the seat to the frame.

Seat foam is not such a big problem, although if it's in good shape, this is a big advantage. Cutting foam to shape is an art and not easy to get right first time, although filling in small holes is a simple task.

1.8 The hinge is in good condition and this seat still has the original cover and chrome edging: a small edge tab can be seen here.

FRAME AND FORKS

Check for obvious damage to the frame and forks: any heavily accident-damaged bike should be avoided, so look in particular for bent components such as forks, swinging arm, stands, footrests, gear and brake levers, as well as dents and deep scratches.

Take a look at the bike head-on and from behind to verify it's square and symmetrical: footrests should be the same height and level with each other. Look especially at the exhaust pipes, as these will be the first to sustain damage if the bike goes over or is dropped, and are easily replaced to conceal this fact. Check the steering head, which should be perfectly round in diameter with no excess play in the bearing: I found one almost oval in shape due to a head-on accident.

Forks should be 100 per cent straight. Replacing stanchions and fork legs is expensive, so check them over thoroughly, and compare with each other. The forks may be twisted in the top and bottom yokes but don't confuse this with them being bent: twisted forks can be easily reset by loosening top and bottom yoke bolts and pulling straight the forks.

If the fork stanchions are rusted and pitted – particularly lower down – it's likely they will need re-chroming or replacing (new stanchions are available). Light rust will polish out, but anything more than that will lead to leaking oil seals. This is not uncommon, and in most cases the oil seals would be changed during a restoration.

It is usual for a bike that has been standing for some time to be low on, if not empty of, fork oil. To test this, push down on the forks and release quickly: if the bike bounces up and down, damping has been lost, and the seals will need replacing and the forks refilling with oil. The oil dampens movement, so there should be very little bounce.

1.9 The forks on this bike are in very good condition, with no sign of oil leakage; the chrome of the stanchion is not showing any corrosion or pitting.

PROJECT ASSESSMENT

The following is a list of parts that I would expect to change or buy on virtually every restoration –

- Piston rings – maybe with a re-bore and new pistons
- Clutch plates – not expensive
- Sparkplugs – always worn
- Contact breaker points – always worn
- Top end gasket set
- Carburettor rebuild kit – original falls apart when stripping carbs
- Brake master cylinder and calliper rebuild kit – almost always seized
- Front brake pads and rear brake shoes
- Brake hoses
- Tyres – always perished
- Inner tubes and rim tape
- Chain and sprocket set – chain always solid; sprocket mostly worn
- Some bulbs
- Seat cover – almost always torn
- Spray paint, including primer filler and abrasive paper
- Decal kit for tank after spraying
- Decal sticker set for frame and side panels, where appropriate
- Oil and filter
- Rubber fuel hoses
- Battery

Combine this list with the parts that you already know are missing and you will have a fair idea of what you will need to buy and what it might cost. The rest is just work – and lots of it: it's worth it in the end, though, believe me!

Chapter 2
Sourcing parts

Once you have purchased your Honda project bike and done your initial assessment, you will quickly build a large shopping list of parts which will grow the further you get into your restoration. So where can you get all of those elusive parts?

THE INTERNET

The internet is undoubtedly the best place to begin looking for parts. Auction websites feature thousands of parts from all over the world, and on websites such as eBay you can often find half a dozen sellers touting the parts you're looking, many of which can be delivered to your door in a few days.

There will often be close-up images of the part concerned, which give a good idea of condition. On the other hand, you can also find vague descriptions and blurry images that do not describe the part properly; be careful if ordering from sellers like this.

If you buy a part from an international seller it's possible you could be charged customs duty when it arrives in your country, and maybe a tax charge, too. All countries have different importation rules so, before buying from an international seller, check what your country's are.

Importing parts is often a good, if not the only, option, but the downside is that you cannot actually see the item you are purchasing, and can only make a true assessment of condition and suitability on delivery. I am UK-resident and have purchased parts from the USA, Germany, France, Japan, and Hong Kong: I've always been happy with what I've bought.

CLUBS AND FORUMS

The benefits of joining a club or forum cannot be over-stressed. These are a great way to source the parts you need, and by joining you will get to know the best and recommended source of parts for your bike.

Many members are marque specialists who have owned and worked on their brand of bike for years. They know every single model and part in minute detail, and can provide new members with invaluable information and advice, from finding parts through fault diagnosis to the easiest way to overcome a problem. You can be sure that members have come across the very same problems that you are likely to encounter, and will already know the simplest solution to resolve them. (Clubs and forums for different marques are listed later in the book.)

For an example of what can be found on the internet, the Honda SOHC forum that I visit has the following sections –

- FAQs
- SOHC archives
- SOHC bikes
- Hondamatic
- High-performance and racing
- Project Shop
- Bike of the month
- Bike and parts sales

Along with these are sections for each and every model of SOHC 4, and a whole lot more. Forums contain a wealth of knowledge which is, in many cases, unrivalled by any other information source, and the above list shows that very little – if anything – is omitted. The references and technical help posts are very good, and the advice given will save you time and money while restoring your bike. There are many forums and clubs for Honda SOHC Fours, and classic motorcycles generally. Some forums and clubs even re-manufacture and supply parts that are no longer available from the manufacturer. If there's enough demand, someone will find a way to manufacture the part required.

SOURCING PARTS

MAGAZINES

Magazines should not be overlooked when it comes to parts supply. At the time of writing, at least eight monthly classic bike magazines were on sale in the UK, most of which are also sold internationally. They all have a classified advert section at the back, along with classic bike dealers with parts for sale. A good source of parts, buying specialist magazines also puts you in touch with experts such as engine rebuilders, chrome platers, sprayers, powder coating companies, and the like.

2.1 A typical stall at an auto jumble, full of interesting parts for sale.

2.0 Bike mags: you'll find features about restoration projects that others have done, plus technical articles and a note of venues and dates for upcoming events such as auto jumbles, classic bike shows, and race meetings.

THE AUTO JUMBLE

The auto jumble or swap meet is my favourite way of sourcing parts. Imagine a market full of stalls selling bikes, parts and accessories just for classics, with thousands of other enthusiasts sifting through boxes, looking for that last little part to finish their project.

Although more time-consuming, at an auto jumble you can at least see the parts on sale, haggle with the seller, and take the part home with you that day; often, the seller will be able to advise you on other parts you may need or other parts they may have at home which are also for sale. And auto jumbles also have bikes for sale, too. Some look like they've just been dragged out of the local river, whilst others are in immaculate condition. Many dealers focus on a particular manufacturer or model, while others will have a mix-and-match approach to their stall. Lots of stallholders are

2.2 Sellers offer useful help and advice – and even the odd sack truck thrown in for heavy objects.

dealers who sell parts and bikes for a living; others have smaller stalls and may just be selling off parts accumulated from old projects over the years. Either way, in my opinion, this is the most enjoyable way to source your parts.

I arrange to meet up with my friends, and we all keep an eye out for what each of us is hoping to find. Refreshments are always available, and you can have a great day out. At the end of the day I load up the car with all my goodies, satisfied I have

2.3 SOHC four parts are usually plentiful at an auto jumble.

HOW TO RESTORE HONDA FOURS

some extra parts to help finish my latest project.

And it's not only used and old parts that are for sale: you'll find stalls selling new fuel pipes, nuts and bolts, badges, stickers, the list is endless.

2.4 A nice selection of old Hondas being inspected by potential buyers.

2.5 11,000 people arrived on a freezing January weekend at a classic bike show in Newark, hoping to find the parts they were looking for.

Chapter 3
Getting started

Before beginning the initial strip down it's a good idea to assess the condition of the engine, especially if you haven't heard it run before. If you can get it running at this stage and all seems okay, it will simply be a case of cleaning and polishing the engine before it is put back in the frame later.

VERY IMPORTANT: Before doing anything with the engine, check the oil level and top up if necessary: don't get caught out by trying to start the engine, only to discover that all of the oil leaked out years ago. The ensuing damage will undoubtedly lead to an expensive repair bill, and can easily be avoided.

Start with basic checks on the ignition and fuel system.

Try turning the key in the ignition: usually an oil or neutral light will come on, but not always.

Give a good kick on the kickstarter or a quick press on the electric start, looking closely at the sparkplug electrode. Does it spark? If it does, great, we're in business and the ignition side is looking good. Check the other sparkplugs in the same way.

If not all of them spark it could be a faulty cap or plug, which you can investigate properly later.

Next check the fuel system (we will assume that the fuel tank is clean). Put in some fresh fuel and pull the fuel hose from the carburettor; turn on the fuel tap and check for fuel coming from it (do this only briefly to determine if the fuel tap is clear). Use a small container to catch any fuel spills.

3.0 With all of my restoration projects I have purchased a new battery: a good quality motorcycle battery will last years.

3.1 Take out one of the sparkplugs and lay it on the cylinder head. Don't hold the sparkplug, hold the plug cap, or it's likely you'll get a shock (this is how I discovered the electrics were okay on my very first project, to the great amusement of my friends!).

3.2 Fuel taps generally have a small filter inside that easily blocks. If fuel comes out, turn off the tap and reconnect the fuel hose to the carburettor. This is a Honda CB350 fuel tap in the 'on' position; also showing 'stop' and 'reserve.'

HOW TO RESTORE HONDA FOURS

Once it's been established that the ignition and fuel areas are okay, we can attempt to start the engine. Do this in an open space, and not inside a garage or shed because exhaust gases are dangerous if inhaled.

If the engine starts let it warm up thoroughly. This may be the first time in years that it has been started, so don't rev it too much, just let it tick over or run at low revs until it is warm. Listen for any strange noises and look for oil leaks. If there are no obvious problems we can assume that the engine is okay, but if, after going through the basic starting check, the engine doesn't start we will investigate why later.

Time to move on to the first stage of the strip down.

STARTING THE STRIP DOWN

It's good practice to make a photographic record of your motorcycle and its parts as you strip it, to refer to when reassembling it at a later stage.

TIP! When dismantling the bike, it's good practice to return screws and bolts to the hole they came out of, if possible. By doing so, not only will you not lose them, but you'll know where they came from, and what their size and type is (you can always exchange for new examples later). Also try and group nuts and bolts: for instance, keep all the engine mounting bolts, washers and nuts together in a small box and label it.

You will find your impact driver very useful here, particularly on engine casing screws. Make sure you use the correct size spanner, socket or screwdriver the first time you attempt to undo something. Attempting to undo a screw or nut with the wrong size tool usually results in a screw or nut becoming rounded, and even more difficult to release. Tools such as bolt extractors can help, should this happen, but far better to remove the item properly, even if some very stubborn examples may require a firm clout with the impact wrench, or warming with a blow lamp.

3.4 When using the impact wrench, hold it firmly on the nut or in the screw so that it does not bounce out when hit. Striking the impact wrench with a club hammer will assist with the turning action required, together with the force necessary to crack the seal of the seized bolt or nut. Often, it's not the thread that is stuck but the head of the nut or screw. I sometimes give casing screws a light sideways tap to help break the seal against the casing, always being careful not to damage the casing, however.

3.3 Start by spraying all nuts, bolts or screws with a light oil such as GT85, which can begin penetrating and help to free any parts that are stuck.

3.5 For nuts such as those used with engine mounting bolts, use a good socket, and hold the other end of the bolt firmly with a suitably-sized spanner (wrench) to prevent it turning. Usually, once the nut begins to move it becomes looser and looser until it comes off, but if it is very tight, apply more light oil as the thread becomes visible, which will also help when it comes to the rebuild.

3.6 Try to organize the bolts and screws into containers and keep them in groups. I place all of the engine mounting bolts in one container separate from other bolts of a similar size so they do not become mixed up. Label the containers.

Begin to remove the larger bike components to allow access to other parts.

GETTING STARTED

Removing the seat and tank

3.7 The seat will usually be held by two clevis pins, each of which has a split pin to retain it in place. Pull out the split pins and put away: you will need them later.

3.8 Remove the clevis pins. These should pull out quite easily, but if not, using a small screwdriver and light hammer, give them a light tap on the end to push them out.

Turn the fuel tap to the 'off' position and unscrew and remove the fuel pipe ready to remove the tank later. Drain the fuel from the tank into a suitable container.

The fuel tank will be held in place by a rubber strap.

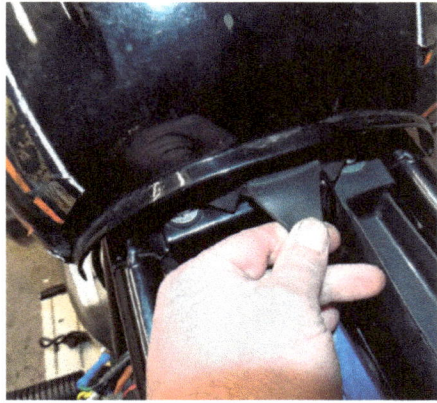

3.9 This tank is held on by a rubber, quick-release strap that pulls off to release the tank.

3.10 Simply pull the tank backward and up a little to free it from the location rubbers hidden under the front of the fuel tank.

3.11 The front of the fuel tank has two brackets that locate on the fuel tank rubbers.

Next, begin removing the side panels, lights, indicators and cables. Try not to damage any electrical connections – always pull the connector, not the wire itself. Remove the entire electrical loom and cables. The latter may be serviceable, and if they look okay it's worth oiling them with light oil as this will help later.

3.12 Do not pull the wires as they may come loose; pull the connector instead.

HOW TO RESTORE HONDA FOURS

Removing the engine
The following procedure describes the basics of removing the engine; more detailed instructions can be found in your workshop manual. Unless you have an engine hoist you'll need someone to help with the lifting.

3.13 Remove the side panels by pulling free from the bottom first, and then popping out the two top lugs.

3.14 Some models have a screw that should be turned 90 degrees to release the panel, which is then unhooked from the top.

3.15 With seat and tank removed, you will be able to see the condition of the wiring, rubbers, and other parts that were covered.

3.16 Remove the split link from the drive chain as shown. Squeezing hard on the split link should cause it to pop off the chain link. If this proves difficult you can also prise off with a screwdriver.

3.17 Disconnect the air filter and remove.

3.18 & 3.19 Remove all carburettors by unscrewing the mounting clamps and disconnecting the throttle and choke cables.

GETTING STARTED

3.20 Remove all exhaust manifolds. These are held in with two nuts. Now remove the complete exhaust system.

3.23 Support the engine with a suitable jack and a piece of wood before removing the engine mounting bolts. The CB750 has no centre stand, so two axle stands were used to steady the bike while removing the engine.

IMPORTANT: The engine is very heavy so, ideally, a suitable engine hoist should be used. In the absence of this or a suitable jack, ensure you have help with lifting out the engine; never attempt it on your own!

3.21 On the CB750 remove the oil tank and hoses. The other models do not have an oil tank.

3.24 Once the engine mounting bolts have been removed, the engine can be lifted out and placed on a strong bench for later inspection.

3.22 Undo all the engine mounting bolts. You'll need two spanners to prevent the bolt from moving while the nuts are undone.

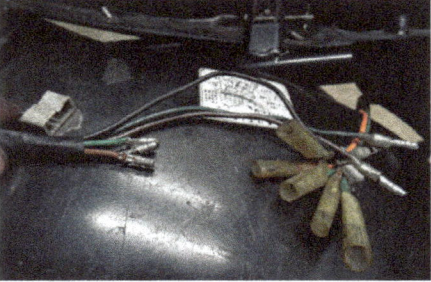

3.25 Disconnect all remaining wires attached to the lights and indicators.

HOW TO RESTORE HONDA FOURS

3.26 Unscrew the nuts and bolts holding the indicators in place. Some screw into the frame and have a locking nut, whilst others screw right through the frame and have a nut and washer on the other end.

3.29 Four nuts and bolts retain the rear mudguard: two at the top, and one each side (which also hold the rear grab rail).

3.27 The chrome is often in poor condition but the indicator stems can be bought separately.

3.30 Undo the two dome-headed nuts that retain the shock absorber, and remove the grab rail. Then pull free the rear mudguard.

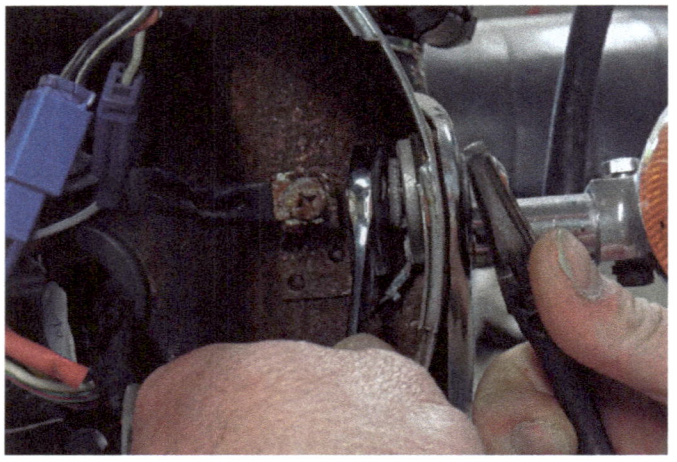

3.28 When unbolting the headlamp, hold the bolt with two spanners to prevent it turning as the nut is undone.

3.31 Now pull out the plastic inner mudguard that locates in two small brackets on the inside of the frame.

GETTING STARTED

3.32 Pull out the split pin and remove the torque arm bolt; remove the bolt at the other end, too.

3.35 Next, remove the split pin from the rear axle nut and unscrew the nut.

3.33 Replace the bolts for safekeeping.

3.36 With the nut removed, pull out the rear wheel axle. This is likely to require a light tap with a rubber mallet on the other end, and you may even need to use an engine mounting bolt to push out the axle completely.

3.34 To push out the rear brake arm shaft a pair of long-nose pliers will be required to unhook the spring underneath.

3.37 Unscrew the remaining bolts and remove the rear shock absorber units.

HOW TO RESTORE HONDA FOURS

3.38 Put the rear wheel adjusters on the axle, along with the nut and spacers, to keep everything together.

3.41 Replace the caps and bolts.

3.39 Mudguards with stays have a further two or four bolts lower down the fork leg. Later mudguards did not have stays.

3.42 Remove all of the smaller parts and keep together for cleaning later.

3.40 Unscrew all of the bolts at the bottom of the forks and pull free the front wheel.

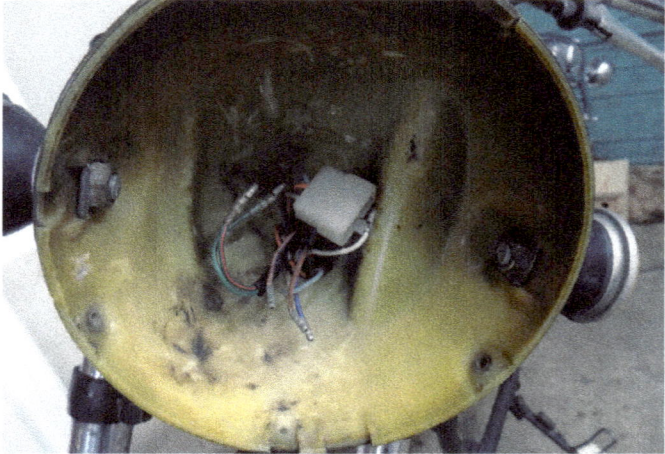

3.43 Remove the headlamp, disconnect the connectors for the handle bar switch gear, and thread through the rear of the headlamp bowl.

GETTING STARTED

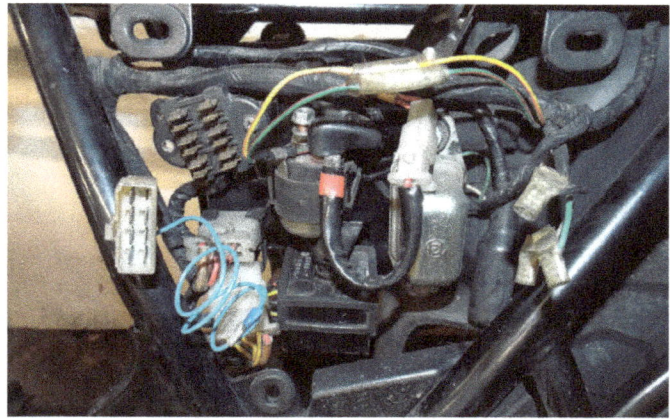

3.44 Now remove the entire loom and electrical panel. It is worth considering a new loom if yours has many bad repairs. Electrical faults are one of the main causes of breakdown.

3.47 Unscrewing the reflectors will reveal the headlamp mounting bolts.

3.45 Remove the switch gear by undoing the screws underneath.

3.47a Unscrew these nuts and remove the headlamp completely.

3.46 Unscrew the four bolts retaining the handlebars

3.48 Loosen the pinch bolts on the upper and lower fork yokes ...

HOW TO RESTORE HONDA FOURS

3.49 ... you'll need to hold both sides on the top bolts ..

3.52 Give a gentle tap with a rubber mallet to help shift the top yoke.

3.50 ... and may need to give a little tap with a rubber mallet to start the forks moving. Then pull free.

3.53 Now unscrew the top bearing holder – you'll need a C-spanner for this.

3.51 Unscrew the large steering stem nut.

3.54 This project bike was already fitted with an aftermarket tapered bearing. This is unusual, and you'll usually find ball bearings here.

GETTING STARTED

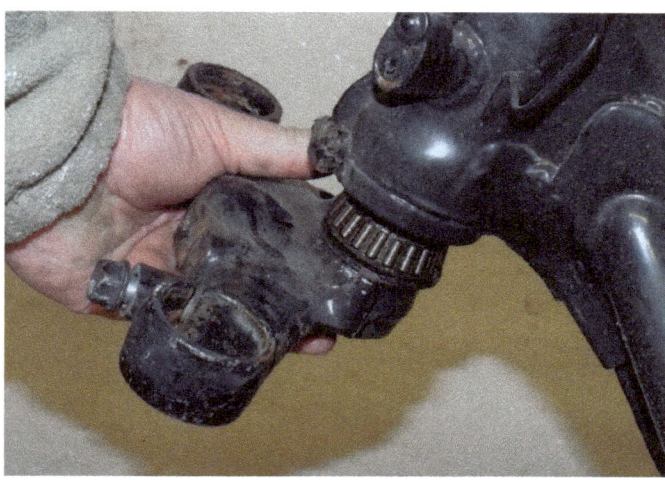

3.55 Slowly pull down the stem, and be prepared for ball bearings to fall out. Try not to lose any; they may be in good condition and reusable.

3.58 Unscrew the large swinging arm nut and withdraw the swinging arm bolt. You'll probably need to tap this out with a hammer and long slim bar or similar.

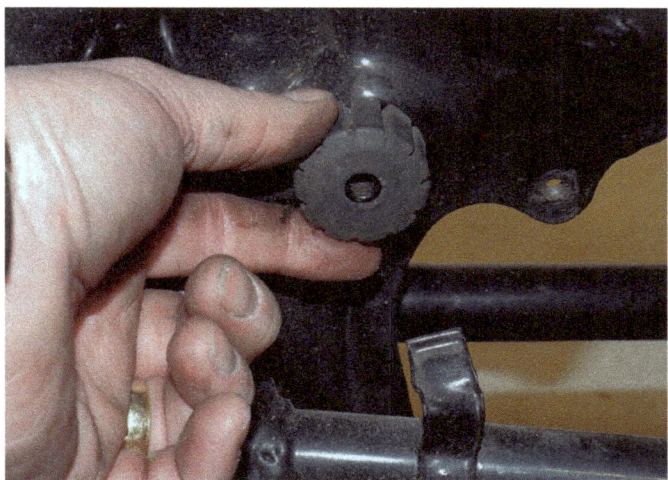

3.56 Remove all rubbers and cable clips.

3.59 A good pair of grips will help pull out the swinging arm bolt.

3.57 Unhook the side stand spring and unbolt the stand; also remove the centre stand, if fitted.

3.60 With everything now removed from the frame, check for cracked welds and other damage.

HOW TO RESTORE HONDA FOURS

3.61 If the old swinging arm bushes are worn, remove them before spraying.

3.62 Also check the rubbers for the shock units, and replace if necessary.

3.63 The area closest to the engine sprocket is likely to be coated in old chain grease, which will require a brush and a good de-greaser to remove.

3.64 After de-greasing the frame, wash off with warm soapy water and then dry.

If intending to spray larger items, begin preparation by applying de-greaser with a small brush, carefully checking for cracks in the frame, which will require welding/brazing.

3.65 De-greased and dried, awaiting preparation.

Once everything is de-greased, flatten off any old scratches or chip marks.

3.66 You will need a selection of different grade wet and dry paper.

GETTING STARTED

3.67 Start with around 120 grade paper to remove the worst of the rust.

3.68 Go over again with a finer grade, such as 240. Make sure the frame is well supported: it will be heavy.

3.69 A multi-tool will save time, and is ideal for sanding those awkward areas. Remove all old stickers at this stage.

Apply tape to protect areas you do not want painted. Replace screws in any threads that you do not want paint getting into.

When spraying, be sure to wear an appropriate protective mask and clothing, as the fumes are toxic.

3.70 A good capacity compressor and spray gun setup are needed if intending to do the spraying yourself ...

3.71 ... but if you don't have this equipment, good results can be achieved with spray can (rattle can) paint. In the case of Hammerite no priming is necessary, and only two coats of the finish gloss are required.

HOW TO RESTORE HONDA FOURS

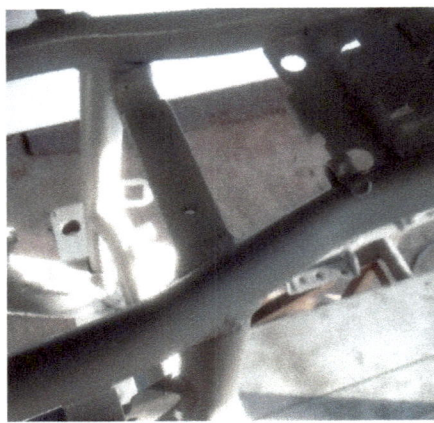

3.72 Spray the entire frame with two coats of primer. Patience is the key with spraying, so ensure each coat is completely dry before applying further coats.

3.73 Suspending smaller parts makes it easier to spray all over them without touching or moving the part.

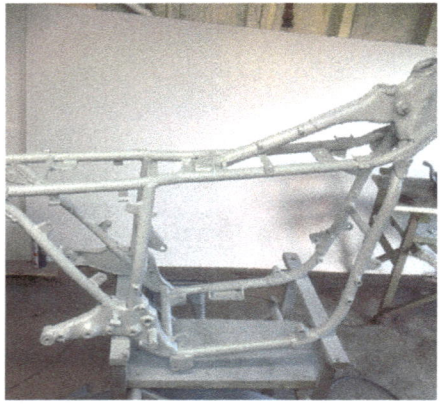

3.74 The complete frame after two coats of primer.

3.75 Apply two coats of the gloss top coats, after which go over the whole frame (or the most visible areas if you want to save time) with a very fine wet and dry paper such as 800-1000 grade. By doing this you will achieve a much shinier gloss finish.

3.76 Spray all black components at the same time. These will be the swinging arm and stands, but can also include engine mounting brackets, the electrical back plate, and the air filter housing.

The frame is now finished and ready for your rebuild.

Chapter 4
Cleaning & polishing

Now that you have a newly-painted or powder-coated frame, it's time to turn your attention to the other parts of the motorcycle. Each must be cleaned and polished to achieve the best possible finish, although some parts may be too rusty or too damaged to salvage, or require sending off for chrome plating.

Thorough cleaning of each part will allow you to assess condition, and establish whether components that have been clogged by years of dust and dirt are in good working order, and/or have the necessary adhesion if they are to be painted/sprayed.

BEFORE YOU START: SAFETY TIPS

• Always use safety equipment – wear a dust mask, safety goggles and gloves at all times
• If using a polishing mop to finish an item, have the mop rotating away from you and hold the item that side of the mop
• Tie back and cover long hair to prevent it becoming caught in machinery
• Fasten loose cuffs and loose clothing. Remove or secure all jewellery
• If the polishing wheel 'grabs' the item being polished, let it go – do not hold on

DE-GREASING

Engine and frame parts will need to be de-greased with a suitable de-greasing agent. Smaller parts can be placed in a bucket and cleaned with a small paint brush, while larger parts – such as the frame – should be cleaned somewhere where the mess this can create won't matter. Standing a frame on end in a large plastic container (such as an old baby bath) against a wall works well, and contains the dirt. De-greaser also has to be rinsed off and the parts dried as soon as possible. This is particularly important with ferrous parts that will quickly rust again if not dried and protected appropriately.

4.1 A freestanding parts washer can be very useful if your budget can stretch to this.

HOW TO RESTORE HONDA FOURS

ULTRASONIC CLEANING

An ultrasonic cleaner is a device that uses ultrasound vibration and an appropriate cleaning solvent (sometimes ordinary tap water) to clean small or delicate items. Many larger cleaners operate up to 80 degrees centigrade. The combination of heat and ultrasonic vibration of around 23,000 kHz is a very effective cleaner. Originally used to sterilise surgical instruments, these machines are now available to buy at reasonable prices. Size is determined by the amount of liquid each can hold, and the dimensions of the basket the parts are held in.

4.2 Smaller items, such as carburettors, can be thoroughly cleaned in ultrasonic cleaners, which come in a variety of sizes. The smaller versions are suitable for cleaning very small parts, such as carburettor jets, whilst larger cleaners can accommodate the whole carburettor. This is, by far, the best way of cleaning carburettors.

4.3 A carburettor before ultrasonic cleaning.

4.4 The same carburettor a few minutes later. Not only is the outside clean but, more importantly, the tiny passageways inside the carburettor body are clean and dirt-free.

CLEANING & POLISHING

EQUIPMENT

4.5 Polishing wheels have been adapted to fit a wide range of garage equipment, the most common of which is the bench grinder.

4.6 With the grinder bolted to a workbench you are able to apply the required pressure to the part being polished.

4.7 One of the grinding wheels is removed and replaced by the polishing mop mandrel, a spiral attachment that allows quick and easy fitting and removal of polishing mop heads. You can also purchase dedicated polishing machines.

4.8 The polishing mop is simply screwed onto the mandrel and the rotation of the spindle holds the mop tightly in place.

4.9 Attachments are also available for pillar drills and hand drills.

METAL POLISHING WHEELS AND COMPOUNDS

Alloy responds well to polishing, and with the correct equipment, it's possible to achieve great results.

Alloy parts, such as fork legs, the engine casing, and control levers, can be polished to a high degree. Polishing kits are great value for money, and come with a selection of polishing wheels and compound bars of different grade polishing wax, which slowly melts away to leave the abrasive to polish/cut the metal. If too much wax is used a residue will be left on the metal surface, which can be removed with white spirit and a clean cloth.

Polishing is much the same as sanding, using progressively finer abrasives, each one 'cutting' the marks left by the previous one. The combination of different grade polishing waxes and polishing mop wheels will leave a high shine finish when the process is complete.

Polishing mops

There are three grades of polishing mop –
- Sisal metal. Very fast cutting and hard, these are used for first stage polishing operations with brown metal polishing compound on soft metals, including aluminium, brass and copper, and black metal polishing compound on hard metals, including steel and stainless steel

HOW TO RESTORE HONDA FOURS

- Colour stitch metal. Versatile cutting mops used for general metal polishing, which can also be used for first stage polishing with brown metal polishing compound on soft metals, including aluminium, brass and copper, or for second stage polishing on hard metals with green, pink and white metal polishing compounds
- Loose fold metal. The most popular, these mops can be used with blue, green, pink, white and rouge metal polishing compounds, and are 100 per cent white soft cotton, with no hard pieces. The mops have centre washers, no staples, and have been finished so they can be used straight away.

Polishing compounds

- Brown – for first cut and flattening on non-ferrous metals
- Blue – for final finishing on non-ferrous metals
- Black – for first cut and flattening on steel
- Green – for final finishing on steel
- Pink – for final, high-polish finishing on chrome and steel
- White – for final, high-polish finishing on stainless steel
- Rouge – for polishing soft precious metals such as gold and silver
- Vienna lime (white powder) – for removing polishing compound and grease residues

The polishing kits will not remove metal, and if parts are heavily scratched, marked or scored, suitable abrasives should be used, such as fine file; wet and dry paper; rubbing blocks.

4.10 Deep scratches in the allow will have to be removed before polishing. Use a fine metal file and file lightly in different directions until the scratch or dent has gone.

4.11 Using wet and dry paper of around 400 grade, sand the filed areas, making sure to regularly dip the paper in a clean water and soap solution: this removes the alloy particles and keeps the paper clean and effective.

Change the wet and dry paper to 600 grade and continue sanding until the marks left by the 400 grade paper have been removed. Continue until you have a completely smooth surface, then clean and de-grease the part prior to polishing.

Begin with the coarser, harder polishing wheel know as Sisal. Once the drill or polisher is rotating, lightly touch the mop head with the grey wax bar, and apply sparingly for two seconds (the dark grey bar is a coarser compound than the white bar and should be used first).

4.12 The piece to be polished should be offered up to the wheel, using medium-to-hard pressure. Go over the whole surface several times until the worst oxidisation has been removed. Always try and vary the direction of the polishing mop over the surface you are polishing, even if by only a few degrees. This may not always be possible, and will depend on the shape of the item being polished. Try to polish across rather than along a scratch.

When all scratches/marks have been removed and the part has a uniform matt finish, remove the sisal metal polishing mop. Note that it is very important to remove all marks/scratches and leave a uniform finish for each grade of wax used.

Re-polish with the softer wheel as before, and go over the whole area of the piece being polished. Patience is the key here. If you require a very highly-polished finish, you'll have to go over the piece with increasingly finer polishing bars until you achieve the shine you want. Then, with a clean cloth, go over the polished article with the white Vienna lime powder, which will remove any grease left on the surface. Buff with a clean cotton cloth to finish.

4.13 The finished fork leg looking as good as new. Polishing can be taken even further for a mirror finish.

Use smaller mops for difficult-to-reach areas.

Chrome polishing

Chrome-plated parts on motorcycles are usually the focus of attention, and it's satisfying when your hard work literally begins to shine. On smaller parts use cream pastes such as Autosol to remove light rust and keep chrome clean.

4.14 A typical indicator in need of a good polish.

CLEANING & POLISHING

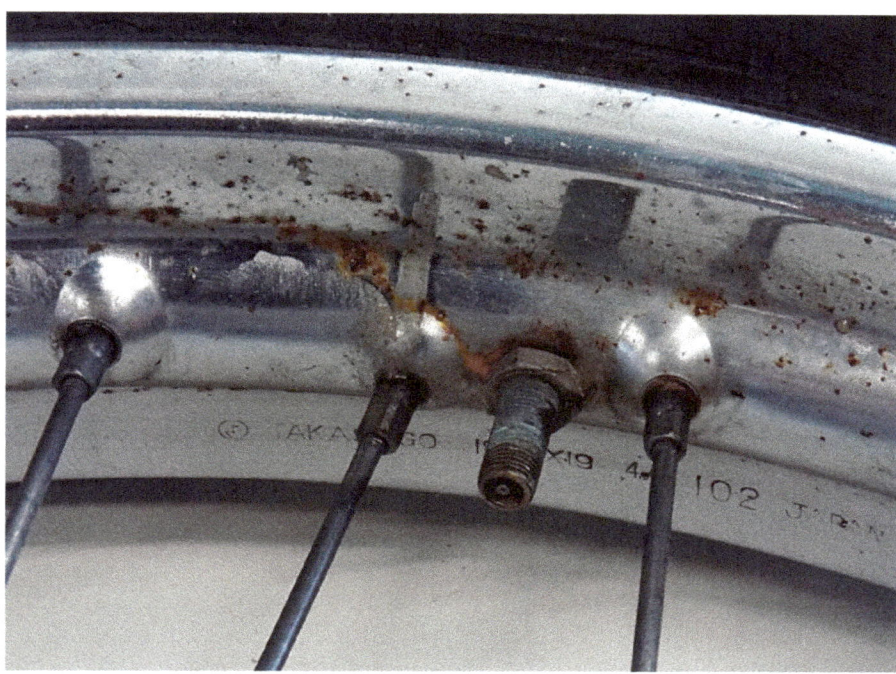

4.15 Light rust on this wheel rim can be easily removed with a suitable chrome polish.

RUST REMOVAL

Inevitably, many parts will have some degree of rust. Some may be completely corroded and no longer usable, whilst others may be in better condition.

Products are available which will remove light surface rust, and can sometimes help loosen rusted parts, or even completely eradicate quite bad rust.

On lightly rusted parts any mild acid – such as vinegar or lemon juice; even Cola – can be used, and soaking the parts overnight in these solutions is the easiest option: allow plenty of time for the parts to soak to get good results.

Larger and more difficult parts should be placed in a bowl – an old plastic baby bath is perfect because it is usually large enough to take most parts from a motorcycle. De-grease the parts and rinse as instructed by the manufacturer.

Many rust removers are concentrated, and can be diluted to make around 20 litres of solution. Most need to be at room temperature to work effectively, and parts are normally left overnight to soak. Follow the instructions supplied with your particular rust remover. Once everything is clean you can decide whether any parts should be sent off for re-plating.

On larger parts use polishing wheels, as you did with alloy parts, but use the soft wheel and fine wax right away. There's no need to use wet and dry paper or the coarser wax as these are too harsh for chrome.

4.16 A good example of some serious polishing on a classic motorcycle. Hard to believe that this bike is almost forty years old!

4.17 After rust has been removed, many parts – such as these bolts – can be buffed on the polishing wheel and reused, but not for your Honda!

33

HOW TO RESTORE HONDA FOURS

4.18 The footrest on the right spent ten minutes in rust remover, after which it had to be thoroughly dried quickly to prevent rust forming again.

After using rust remover, rinse the cleaned part, dry and spray with a light oil such as GT85 to prevent rust returning.

More heavy-duty rust or paint removal could necessitate the use of a shot-blasting cabinet, such as the one in 4.19. This piece of kit runs on compressed air supplied by a compressor, and blasts different grades of media, such as recycled crushed glass of crushed walnut shells, at high pressure onto the piece being cleaned, removing all rust back to bare metal. These cabinets are commonly used to clean engine crank cases, heads and barrels.

4.19 A small cabinet blaster will be an asset to your workshop. It connects to a compressor and has a blast gun inside the cabinet. Different grades of blast media can be used in the cabinet. The item is placed inside, where rust and dirt is blasted off. The media is recycled inside the cabinet and can be used several times. This is a dry process and any item that requires this treatment should be free from grease.

4.20 The exhaust port on a cylinder barrel requires cleaning before a rebuild.

4.21 This is the same cylinder barrel after a few minutes in the blasting cabinet, with all carbon deposits now removed. This is a quick, clean process, recommended for cleaning numerous motorcycle parts prior to refitting.

CLEANING & POLISHING

Before I purchased my first blast cabinet I enquired about having some parts cleaned. The price I was given for blasting two parts was more than half the cost of buying the blasting cabinet! Although the blast cabinet is an effective tool for cleaning heavily soiled and rusted parts, proceed with caution when it comes to soft alloys and other delicate surfaces. These cabinets are powerful, and you must use the correct blast media according to the surface being blasted. For a motorcycle side stand made of steel, for example, a coarse media such as iron could be used, whilst for a cylinder barrel, as in 4.21, crushed walnut shells should be used as these are much softer and won't damage the part.

DIY chrome plating

Many parts on the SOHC Fours are chrome plated, which gives a pleasing appearance and protects the base metal underneath. A polished, finished bike is the pride and joy of its owner, who may spend hours polishing it. Unfortunately, road grime and salt can take their toll on chrome plating over the years, resulting in rusty, pitted areas.

Several options are available if this is the case with your bike. You can polish these areas with off-the-shelf chrome polish, or, if the part is too badly corroded, replace it with a good condition, secondhand part.

You can also send your part to be re-chromed: many companies offer this service, and the results can be very good with the finished article looking like new. This is by far the best option, albeit not the cheapest.

Failing the above, you could try DIY chrome plating. Kits have become more readily available over the last few years, and can give (with a little patience and practice) acceptable results. Most DIY kits are intended for use on smaller bike parts, such as brackets, nuts, bolts and spindles, which all add to overall appearance. The dome bolts that retain handlebar clamps; the heads of the nuts and bolts that locate the front and rear mudguards (fenders) are in full view – and always in chrome.

Replica chrome plating kits give a finish good enough to satisfy the average restorer, and can be quite easy to use, running off a simple, small car battery charger, and relatively inexpensive to buy. They do not take up much room and – you'll like this bit – will save you money in the long run. Some chemicals are involved, but all kits come with instructions which include safety advice. Instructions for use can often be found on the manufacturer's website: read these beforehand to help you decide if this option is suitable.

Chapter 5
The engine

In this chapter we will be dismantling, repairing and rebuilding a CB750 engine: an engine previously unknown to me, so together we will discover the good, the bad, and possibly the ugly of this Honda engine. If faults are found (and they usually are), we will discover why they occurred, and what can be done to rectify them and prevent them recurring. Faults with this engine can also occur on any Honda SOHC unit, and the strip down and rebuild process is very similar.

Problems I've come across in the past – not necessarily on Hondas but which occur with SOHC engines – are mentioned as they are relevant. Use a workshop manual in conjunction with this chapter as the former will give precise torque settings that will be needed when rebuilding the engine.

5.0 A Honda CB750 single overhead cam 4-stroke with 4 carburettors and a 4-into-4 exhaust system. Originally introduced in 1969, this bike is recognized as a milestone in motorcycle history, and often called the first superbike. Honda produced many 4-cylinder, road-going motorcycles with essentially the engine seen here, the range including the CB350F, CB400F, CB500F, CB550F and CB650, right up to the CB750.

THE ENGINE

ENGINE UNIT

5.1 This chapter gives a step-by-step guide to stripping and rebuilding a CB750 engine, although most of the information is relevant to any other SOHC Honda Four. Where other engine sizes differ, this will be highlighted. Rebuilding the engine should be carried out in conjunction with a workshop manual that provides measurements, adjustments, and torque settings specific to your model. With the correct tools, many tasks are not difficult for an enthusiastic restorer.

5.2 However, once we take a closer look we soon start to find problems. Here, a screw has been snapped off, and an attempt made to drill it out.

5.3 Damaged fins: generally, fin damage is only a cosmetic issue and does not affect engine performance, unless the fins are severely damaged, which could lead to engine cooling problems. Damaged fins will certainly affect the resale value of your motorcycle.

5.4 Damaged threads and heads: it's likely you'll come across damaged threads, and bolt or screw heads on your project. These are repairable, and how to deal with these is detailed later in the book. The main one to check is the sparkplug thread: if this is very badly damaged it could mean a machine shop fix, which is a little expensive.

Although some work may need to be carried out by a motorcycle engineer because of the precision machining required, there are many tasks that you can do, potentially saving yourself money. The feeling you get when you first fire up an engine that you have built and set up is great; better still, if you have gone to the trouble of carrying out your own rebuild and anything does go wrong at a later date, you will have the know-how to resolve the problem much more quickly.

What you will need

It's advisable to change certain parts – some service, some mechanical – on all engines during a restoration project.
• Gasket set. Always buy a full engine gasket set, even if you do not always strip the whole engine. The spare gaskets and seals will come in useful later, and buying the bigger gasket set is more cost-effective than buying individual gaskets. Some seals are not included in all gasket sets, so check and try to get hold of these separately, if needed
• Remember that you will also need to fill the engine with fresh oil when you rebuild it. Buy the oil recommended by the manufacturer. Don't forget a new oil filter
• Sparkplugs and air filter
• Clutch plates. These are consumable parts that do wear during normal use. Clutch plates are not expensive, easy to source, and not difficult to replace

These are general procedures common to all SOHC engines. Refer to the user manual for your specific model when carrying out the following tasks.

What to look for on an external inspection: this can be checked with the engine still in the frame.

HOW TO RESTORE HONDA FOURS

5.5 Kickstart and gearbox shafts: check that these have good splines. Often, the kickstart or gear change shaft has a badly worn spline, which will require replacement because it's not easy to repair properly, or while the shaft is still inside the engine.

5.7 Externally, this engine looks in pretty good condition. Make sure you drain the oil into a suitable container before removing the side covers.

5.8 Remove side covers to access parts of the engine, such as the clutch and ignition mechanism.

Once the clutch side cover is off, expect all parts to look reasonably clean, as seen here. A visible film of oil should cover the clutch components, with all mechanical parts looking sound. Look for broken metal pieces in the bottom of the housing, visible breaks and obvious damage. All internal nuts and bolts should be in very good condition: any damaged elements should be replaced.

5.6 Damaged casings or crank case. Check for cracks and oil leaks: cracks can be repaired if not too large, although this is not how a repair should look.

Engine out

With the engine safely on your bench and cleaned with a suitable de-greaser you can begin your inspection. First, take a good look at the engine. Do you notice any cracks or leaks? Any screws or bolts with damaged threads? There are almost always some, and you will have to get these out before you can proceed with the internal inspection.

What you find now will give a good basic idea of what you are likely to come across when stripping and rebuilding, and what to look out for while doing so.

5.9 Unscrew the bolts equally, a little at a time, so that the clutch lifter plate comes off evenly. Behind the plate you will find four clutch springs.

THE ENGINE

5.10 In the centre is a special clutch locknut, behind which is a spring washer (smaller models have a large spring clip/circlip instead). Once this is removed the clutch hub can be pulled free.

5.11 To remove the locknut you will need a special tool, which is not expensive and will save you time when dismantling the clutch. You will find that when you try to undo this nut the clutch turns.

5.12 With the clutch hub and plates removed, all that's left is the clutch outer basket. Check this for damage, and also check below it for any signs of swarf, indicating damage. On some models this basket will pull off easily, and on others will require a puller to remove.

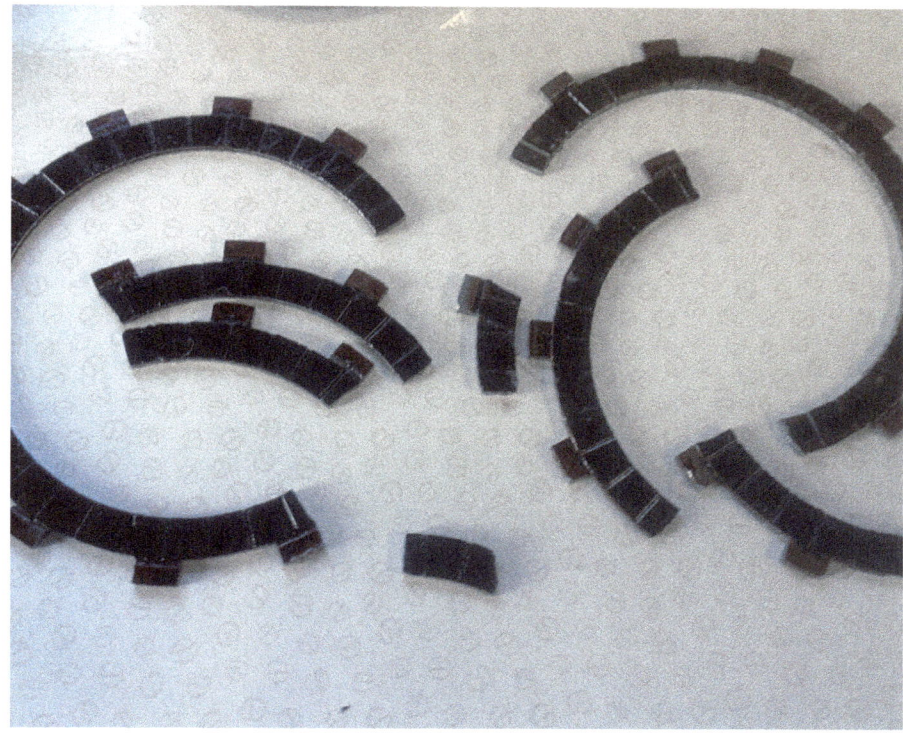

5.13 After removing one clutch basket the clutch plates were found in pieces. Some smaller pieces were discovered in the bottom of the clutch housing.

The colour of the oil will give a good indication of the engine's internal condition. The oil should have the colour of rich honey, and be clear, not milky white or black-looking. It should be smooth to the touch and not gritty.

5.14 If the oil is milky-looking, as here, water has penetrated the engine, most likely via a bad gasket or faulty seal. Identify the exact cause and rectify before rebuilding the engine.

HOW TO RESTORE HONDA FOURS

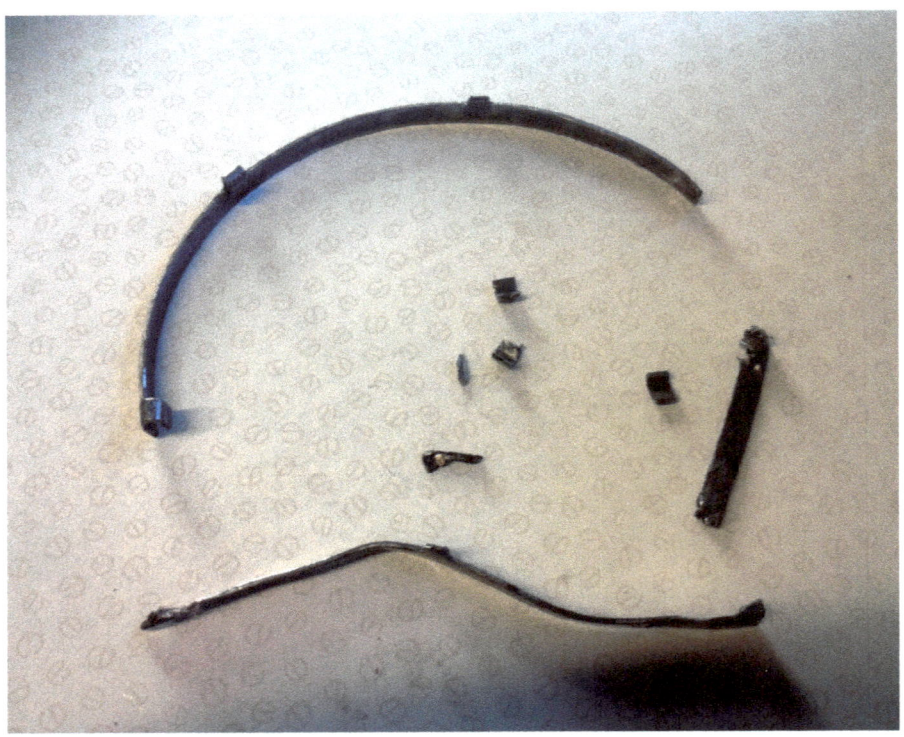

5.15 Broken clutch basket parts found after the side cover was removed.

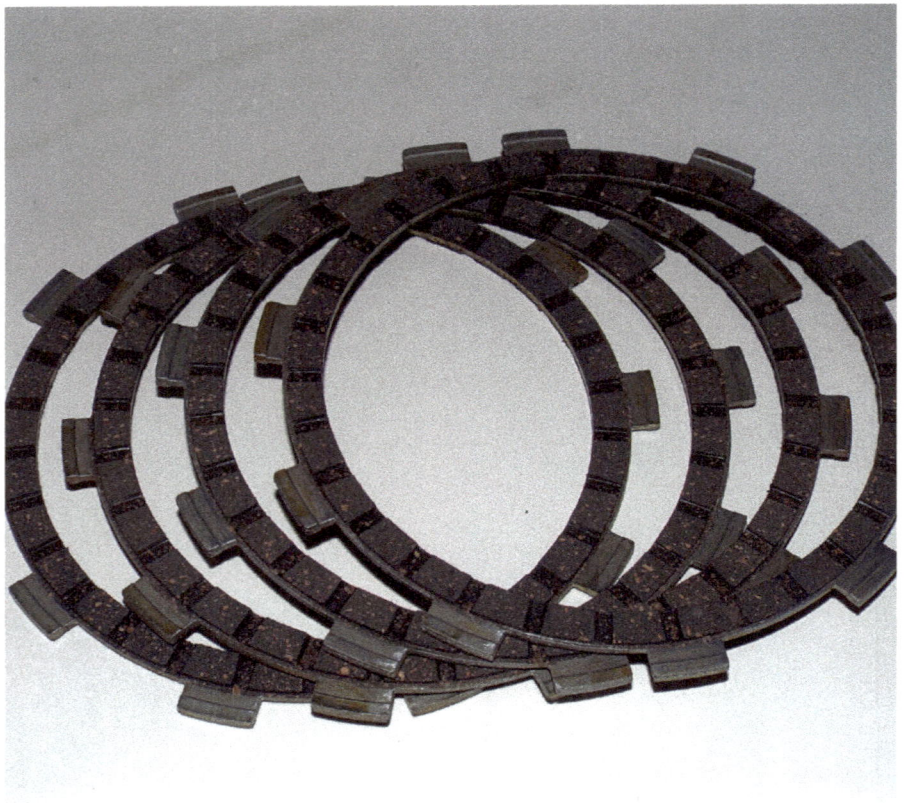

5.16 Replacing clutch plates is a very easy task, and with a new set of clutch plates being relatively inexpensive, I recommend always replacing the old plates.

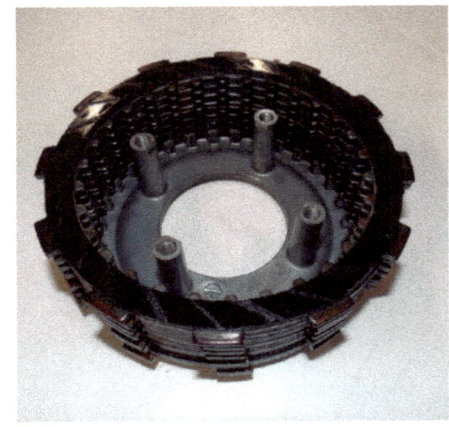

5.17 New clutch plates fitted to the clutch basket.

Now we can turn our attention to the other side of the engine.

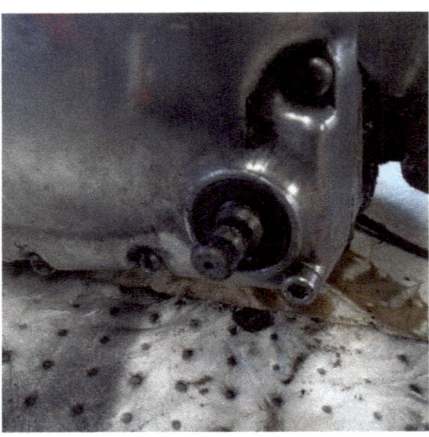

5.18 Remove the gear lever. Note the oil absorbent sheet. Despite draining the oil there will always be some left inside the side casing that will end up on your bench. Have some cloth ready to mop it up.

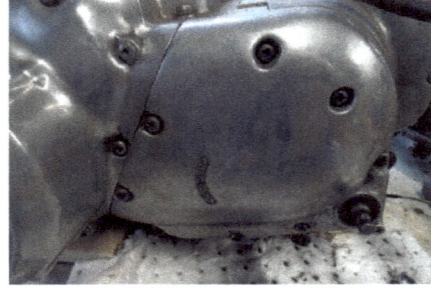

5.19 Unscrew all side casing screws and remove the side casings. Be careful here, and be aware of wires that pass through parts of the casing. Underneath here is the neutral light switch wire that should be unscrewed.

THE ENGINE

5.20 Removing the side casings will allow access to the generator and the ignition. Feel for end play (lash) in the crankshaft by pulling and pushing it from each end. There should be no sideways movement: if there is, this indicates worn bearings which must be corrected. As this is not normally easy to do, it's recommended that a professional do the job (covered at the end of this chapter).

Cylinder head and barrels
The cylinder head can be unbolted, and, once removed, the true condition of the engine will be evident. Removing the head will reveal the cylinder bores, the piston crowns, and the underside of the cylinder head itself. Remember that the head bolts should be undone in the pattern shown in your workshop manual, and re-tightened the same way, and to a particular torque setting. You will need a torque wrench to do this, and the torque settings will be listed in your workshop manual.

5.22 Start by removing the breather cover, which will reveal other bolts that need to be removed.

5.23 Follow this by removing all of the rocker cover screws, and pull free the rocker cover.

5.21 Removing the rotor nut is difficult because it is highly torqued: an assistant will be useful here to hold the engine and help prevent the crankshaft rotating. A special rotor removal tool is recommended by Honda for removing the rotor. This simply screws into the centre of the rotor.

HOW TO RESTORE HONDA FOURS

5.24 With the rocker cover off, we can now see the cam chain, camshaft with sprocket, and rockers. On the CB750 the three bolts on each of the four rocker shafts have to be removed in order to withdraw the rocker shafts. This is not necessary on smaller engines because the rockers are housed within the rocker cover.

5.27 Undo the three bolts holding the cam chain tensioner in place and remove this. On smaller models, loosen the cam chain tensioner underneath the carburettors (on some early models it is at the front of the engine by the exhaust downpipes above the oil filter housing).

5.25 The CB350 cylinder head with rocker cover removed, showing camshaft, cam chain and valves. Note on this engine that the rocker cover also houses the cam bearing cap and the rockers.

5.28 The object of both these procedures is to allow some slack in the cam chain in order to withdraw the camshaft. On the smaller engine, the small bolts (there are two) which hold the camshaft sprocket also have to be removed in order to withdraw the camshaft.

5.26 This tappet locknut was found to be completely loose, which is very unusual. Others were also found to be loose, and tappet clearance was incorrect on many of the valves.

5.29 Turn the engine with the large nut at the ignition end of the crankshaft.

THE ENGINE

5.30 Align the timing index mark horizontally, as shown here, with the groove at the top. Note that the numbers stamped in the camshaft carrier and top caps are matching pairs, and should be replaced in the same formation. This is not the case on the smaller engined models where the camshaft top caps are an integral part of the rocker cover.

5.31 Remove the camshaft carrier caps.

5.32 On all models it is important to support the cam chain while removing the cam, head and barrels, as shown on this CB350 engine. Do not let the cam chain fall into the centre of the engine. A little tension should be kept on the cam chain so that it does not come off of the crankshaft sprocket below.

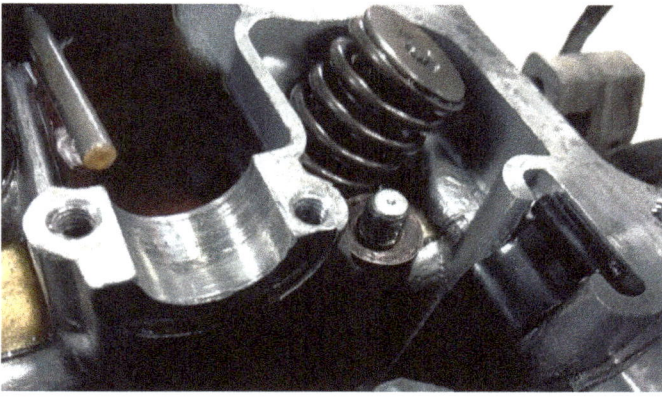

5.33 All models have plastic cam chain guides that can be pulled free.

5.34 After removing the third cap it was obvious why this bike had been abandoned: the camshaft had snapped in two.

5.35 This is serious damage, though rare, thankfully.

HOW TO RESTORE HONDA FOURS

5.36 The camshaft bearing is very badly worn and will need replacing. Luckily, the camshaft carrier can be unbolted from the cylinder head on this model.

5.39 Remove all cylinder head nuts in the order given in your shop manual.

5.37 The unexpected 'double overhead camshaft,' or rather the two halves of the broken camshaft.

5.40 Four nuts are hidden inside the head.

5.38 Once the camshaft carriers are removed replace the rockers and rocker shafts for safekeeping.

5.41 The crosshead screws are very well hidden underneath rubber seals, and are easily missed. I strongly advise replacing these with cap head bolts (Allen bolts) because these are much less likely to be a problem to remove at a later date. If a crosshead screw is difficult to remove it will be difficult to repair.

THE ENGINE

Once all of the nuts and bolts have been removed, gently tap around the edges of the cylinder head to help loosen it. Do not hit the cylinder head fins, as these are fragile and will break easily.

You may find that, once the head has been removed, all that's required is a de-coke and clean, although, often, you will find worn valve stem seals and poorly seating valves. Anything worse than that usually means a trip to the local engineering shop for a head rebuild.

If you fancy tackling reseating the valves yourself, though, you'll need to remove them from the head. Ideally, they should be kept so that they can be returned to the same seat from which they were removed.

5.42 Use a valve spring compressor to compress the valve spring sufficiently to remove the collets.

5.44 Once the collets have been removed, the valve stem seals are visible. Renew all of these seals.

5.43 With the valve spring compressed, use a small magnet to lift out the collets.

5.45 Remove the valve stem seal and pull out the valve. Repeat this for all valves and keep all valves, springs and collets, etc, in a safe place.

HOW TO RESTORE HONDA FOURS

5.46 The collets, valve springs, and stem seal.

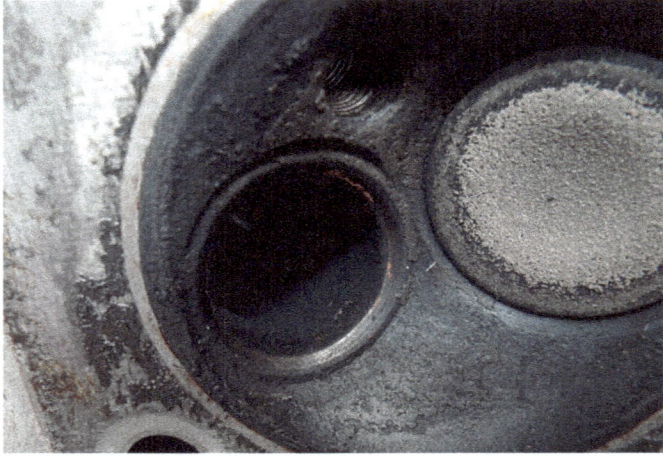

5.47/5.48 Valve seats as bad as this will require machining as will the valves, prior to a final lapping with grinding paste. It is important to remove all traces of lapping paste before re-assembly.

5.49 A valve being refaced at an engineering workshop.

5.50 One of the valves after refacing and just requiring lapping into its valve seat, which has also been refaced.

5.51 After the valve and seat have been lapped-in with grinding paste, refit the valve with new stem seal and replace the collets with a small pair of tweezers. Repeat this with all of the valves, and you will have a rebuilt head.

Once all the valves have been reseated, the reassembly procedure is the reverse of dismantling.

THE ENGINE

5.52 Remember to replace the seals: inside two of the seals is an oil control orifice that looks like a small aluminium peg with holes in.

5.54 The head off, showing the cylinder bores. In this case the bores had to be re-bored due to wear and scoring.

5.53 This piston has carbon build-up, but notice the two small marks left by the exhaust valve slightly touching the piston. It's very likely the valve will need to be replaced because it could be bent. However, the marks on the piston seem to have affected the carbon only and not the piston itself. Further investigation will be required here.

Now is a good time to de-coke the cylinder head by simply removing all old carbon deposits until back to the metal. Try not to scratch the head while removing the carbon.

Try not to let anything drop into any of the cylinder bores or in the cam chain tunnel: use some clean cloth to block the bore whilst inspecting it. If something does drop into the cam chain tunnel it will find its way into the engine crankcase, necessitating a major engine strip down.

Check whether bores are scratched or scored. Check the gap between the piston and the cylinder (the tolerances will be in your workshop manual). The piston crown should be tan in colour; this gives an indication of how rich or lean the engine was running. Too dark and the engine is running too rich; too light and the engine is running too lean. An engine that is running too lean can seize, so it really is important to check this and set the fuel mixture correctly.

If there's no indication of crankshaft problems – such as with the seals or bearings – you need go no further with the strip down. Honda SOHC engines are robust, and, if serviced regularly, go a long time before major engine work is required.

Once bores and pistons have been checked, progress to the next step and remove the cylinder block if necessary. If the bores were found to be satisfactory, you are lucky and there's no need to remove the cylinder block.

Slowly pull up the cylinder block. If stuck firm, a gentle tap all round with a rubber mallet usually does the trick of freeing the block. Try to tap somewhere solid; not on any of the cooling fins because these are easily damaged.

Once you have broken the seal and the cylinder block starts to rise, as previously, don't let anything drop into the crankcase. Use more clean cloth – and be careful!

Now continue to lift the cylinder block, noting that the pistons will be at different heights to each other. You may need an assistant here because it is necessary to lift the block whilst at the same time holding the connecting rod (conrod) that is being exposed, which will prevent the piston flopping over and hitting the barrel studs.

HOW TO RESTORE HONDA FOURS

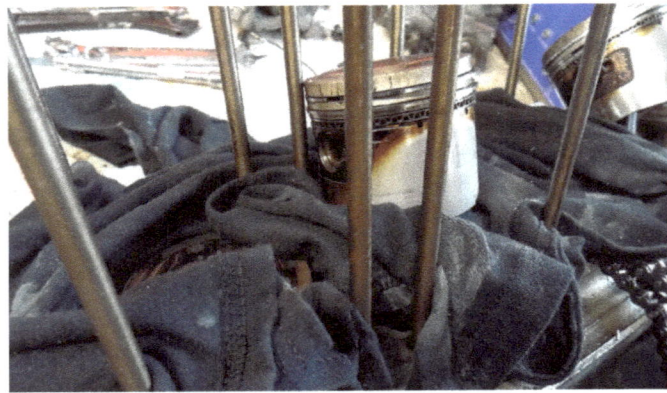

5.55 Once the cylinder block is fully removed use a clean cloth to prevent debris falling into the crankcase. Now check the piston rings and properly measure the piston itself. You'll also be able to gauge whether there is any play in the big and small end bearings (there should be no play – movement up and down – in the bearings). If there is play, renew the small end bearing, or replace the bearing shells if it's the big end: speak to your motorcycle engineer about this.

5.56 You may find that the piston rings are worn or broken and need replacing. This piston is showing signs of wear, and also exhaust gasses have started to blow past the piston rings.

5.57 To remove the piston pull out the small spring clip with a pair of long-nose pliers. This is a simple task, but hold the spring firmly as it can spring out if held too loosely. That being the case, it may be a good idea to wear safety glasses because these clips spring out at quite a speed, and could hit you in the eye.

5.58 There are two spring clips but you need remove only one. Once removed, use a thin tool such as a screwdriver to push out the gudgeon pin (this should push out easily).

5.59 Push the gudgeon pin far enough out to release the piston.

5.60 Repeat the procedure on all four pistons.

THE ENGINE

The bottom end

I mentioned previously that it may not be necessary to carry out a bottom end rebuild – and, in any case, much of this task would have to be undertaken by a professional engineer – but we will cover a bottom end strip down for those who suspect some work is required in that area.

Bottom end engine rebuilds are only carried out if there are problems with the crankshaft, such as main bearings or big end bearings. Other bottom end work could involve gears or seals. Main engine crankcases have to be taken apart to allow access to these areas.

5.61 On top and underneath the crankcases are 10mm and 12mm bolts. Unscrew all bolts in the top half of the crankcase.

5.62 Place all the bolts in order in a piece of cardboard so that they are refitted in the correct places.

5.63 Turn over the engine to reveal the engine sump (oil pan) cover and the other crankcase bolts.

5.64 Removing the sump cover allows access to the oil pump. Here, you can see that the oil strainer has done what it is designed to do and prevented the swarf particles from the damaged cam and cam carrier recirculating around the oil system.

5.65 Three x 10mm bolts hold the oil pump in place.

HOW TO RESTORE HONDA FOURS

5.66 With the bolts removed, pull free the oil pump.

5.69 Remove the three crosshead screw to access the inner and outer pump rotors.

5.67 Once the oil pump has been removed, clean the pump body and strainer with de-greaser.

5.70 Measure the clearance between the inner and outer rotors and also between the outer rotor and the pump body, and check the measurements against your workshop manual.

5.68 Remove the oil strainer and blow through with an airline to expel all debris.

5.71 Do not lose the three dowels. Note the three O-rings which must be replaced with new items.

THE ENGINE

5.72 Dismantle all oil pump parts and clean. When reassembling, place the pump in a container of oil until completely covered, and rotate the pump drive gear. This fills the pump with oil ready for the first start-up after your rebuild.

5.73 Replace the strainer and store the pump safely until you are ready for the rebuild.

5.73a Continue to remove the remaining crankcase bolts, placing them through a piece of cardboard as shown before.

5.74 While taking your engine apart you will come across locating dowels. Some will have a rubber seal (these need to be renewed) and others won't. Store the dowels safely, and remember where they go: these are important when putting everything back together. When you lift off the bottom crankcase, some of these could drop out, so take care not to lose them.

Once all the crankcase bolts are removed, give a gentle tap around the sides of the crankcase with a rubber mallet to loosen the two halves. Find a solid part of the crankcase to tap, and avoid hitting thin areas that could crack (I tap the engine mounting castings).

5.75 It may be the case that you find a damaged piston, so splitting the engine to get to the crankcase is necessary. In this photo, parts from a broken piston skirt must be removed before we can successfully rebuild the engine ...

HOW TO RESTORE HONDA FOURS

5.76 ... this is quite involved and means removing the clutch, the gears, the kick- and electric start mechanisms, along with other components.

5.77 While holding the primary chains, lift out the transmission main shaft and remove; then set the shaft aside for later inspection.

Now lift out the complete crankshaft by passing it through both the primary and camshaft chains.

5.78 With the crankshaft removed you can now see the condition of the main bearing shells. Don't forget the other half of the main bearing shell in the crankcase that was removed. Check all for signs of wear and replace if necessary.

5.79 This leaves the transmission gears and kickstart mechanism.

Although it is not often that there is a problem with the gears, I still remove them so that I can thoroughly clean everything and inspect the crankcase for more debris.

5.80 Pull out the gearshift fork shaft, remembering the fork positions and that one fork sits above the gears.

THE ENGINE

5.81 I check the forks then put them back on the shaft in the correct order until I am ready to refit them.

5.84 Pulling the gears to the side allows room on the opposite end of the shaft to release two large gears.

5.82 To remove the gearshift drum, first remove the neutral switch located in the lower crankcase ...

5.85 Remove the gears ...

5.83 ... and pull free the gearshift drum.

5.86 ... and pull out the shaft with the remaining gears.

HOW TO RESTORE HONDA FOURS

5.87 Much more debris is now visible, but we now have easy access for cleaning. The kickstart mechanism is held in with a steel pin which, once removed, allows the shaft to be pulled free and the gear lifted out.

5.88 Several bearing set rings sit in grooves in the crankcase. These are easy to miss and lose, so follow the same advice as that given for the engine locating dowels. Clean the grooves before refitting the set rings.

5.89 Lots of alloy particles were found in the bottom of the crankcase, which, alone, justifies the complete strip down. This swarf would cause considerable damage to the engine if not removed.

5.90 Clean off old jointing compound and gasket with a flat, sharp blade. Try not to damage the alloy surface while doing this.

Then there's the crankshaft itself. This could well need the main bearings re-grinding (carried out in an engine workshop by a professional).

5.91 The complete crankshaft with conrods still in place.

Once the engine is fully stripped, replace all seals and gaskets and inspect parts such as the gears, clutch, etc, as you go. If you fall into the 'not so confident with engines' category, you may want to let the professionals carry out bottom end work.

THE ENGINE

5.92 You should now have two empty crankcases. Thoroughly de-grease, wash and dry these. There should be absolutely no dirt, grease or particles of any sort left in the crankcase when cleaning is finished. Clean out any oil passages and any hole that you can see – blow through with an airline if you have one.

5.93 Check, or ask your workshop to check, the crankshaft journals before beginning your rebuild.

5.94 If you have any doubts about the big end bearings, remove the conrods by unscrewing the two nuts at the bottom ...

5.95 ... and inspect the big end shells for wear. Note that each cap and rod are a matched pair.

REBUILDING THE ENGINE

With everything now clean and refurbished, you can start the engine rebuild. Prepare a clean working space and get together everything required for the rebuild: all new or refurbished parts, some silicone, jointing compound, seal and gaskets.

5.96/5.97 You will need a full gasket set and a new set of seals and rubbers.

HOW TO RESTORE HONDA FOURS

5.98 Begin by refitting the kickstart and gear assembly in the reverse order of removal.

5.101 Replace the dowels and seals.

5.99 Make sure the ends of the forks slot into the drum.

5.102 Replace the primary and camshaft chains on the crankshaft.

5.100 Use a light smear of assembly grease on the main bearing shells before replacing the crankshaft.

5.103 Carefully lift the whole crankshaft assembly and lower into the crankcase as shown ...

THE ENGINE

5.104 ... remembering to fit the new seal on the end of the crankshaft.

5.107 Refit the final driveshaft with a new seal.

5.105 Refit the gearbox main shaft.

5.108 Use a jointing compound on the mating surface of one half of the crankcase: I spread this thinly, using my finger to dab all over these areas.

5.106 The centre fork locates on this shaft.

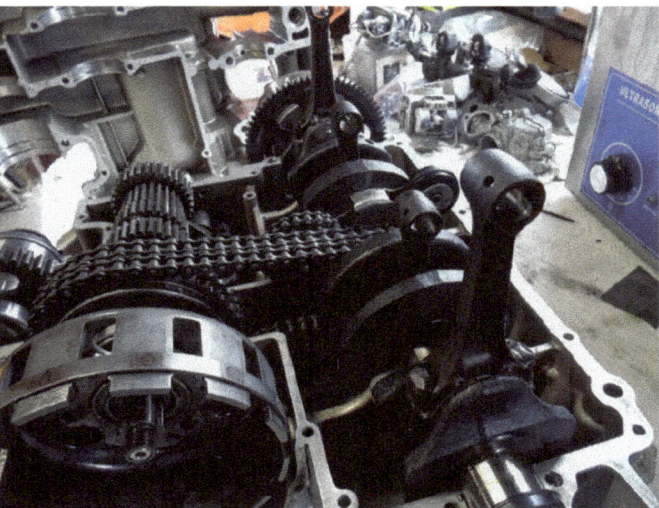

5.109 Stand up the conrods and lower the top half of the crankcase onto the bottom half.

HOW TO RESTORE HONDA FOURS

5.110 You may need some help while lowering the top half of the crankcase and passing through the cam chain (retain the cam chain with some wire).

5.113 Replace the crankcase bolts and tighten to the torque setting given in your workshop manual.

5.111 Give a gentle tap with a rubber or wooden mallet to firmly seat the two halves of the crankcase on the dowels.

5.114 Now turn over the engine.

5.112 Refit the cam chain tensioner.

5.115 Replace the crankcase bolts and tighten to the torque settings given in your workshop manual.

THE ENGINE

5.116 The oil pump should be primed before fitting. Honda advises that the pump be immersed in oil and turned until it is filled with oil; I also ensure that ALL parts are well lubricated before refitting.

5.117 Now refit the sump cover using a new gasket, and replace the neutral switch.

5.118 Return the engine to an upright position.

5.119 Replace the countershaft bearing holder.

5.120 Replace the stopper plate and rollers.

5.122 Next, replace the drum and arm stopper, making sure that the springs are fitted in the correct locations. Both stoppers should be under tension.

5.121 Bolt on the shift stopper.

5.123 Lastly, replace the gear shift spindle.

THE ENGINE

5.124 Replace the engine drive chain sprocket.

5.126 Build the clutch centre with the clutch plates, starting with a friction plate ...

5.125 Refit the reduction gear. The shaft goes into a hole in the generator cover.

5.127 ... and alternate between plane and friction plates until the centre is built up.

5.128 Lastly, fit the clutch pressure plate.

5.130 Slide the clutch plate assembly into the clutch basket.

5.129 Refit the clutch basket, remembering to fit the spacer and circlip after the basket is on the shaft.

5.131 Place the locking (tab) washer on the shaft.

THE ENGINE

5.132 Screw on the lock nut and, after tightening, bend over the tabs of the locking washer so that they sit inside the locknut grooves, as shown.

5.134 Insert the clutch plate lifter and screw in the four bolts. You will need to push back the plate so that you can get the bolts started on their threads. Once you have them started, tighten a few turns of each nut in sequence so that the plate is pulled back evenly.

5.133 Place the four springs inside the clutch.

5.135 Slide on the ignition advancer.

63

HOW TO RESTORE HONDA FOURS

5.136 Replace the contact breaker backing plate. If you marked the plate before removing, align the marks (this will save setting up the timing later).

5.138 Replace the clutch cover; use a new rubber seal on the kickstart shaft.

5.137 Lastly, fit the adjuster nut, which is used to rotate the engine when setting up valve and ignition timing.

5.139 Replace the rotor and tighten the bolt to the torque setting given in your workshop manual.

THE ENGINE

5.140 When tightening the rotor nut, lock the crankshaft by inserting a gudgeon pin and a strong piece of wood, and slowly rotating the crankshaft until the gudgeon pin sits on the wood (ensure nothing drops into the crankcase).

5.142 Insert one of the spring clips before offering up the piston to the conrod. This way, when you inset the gudgeon pin it will stop in the correct position.

5.141 If fitting new pistons put on the piston rings with the gaps set at 120 degrees to each other, and the oil scraper ring at the bottom.

5.143 Lower the piston over the conrod, arrow mark facing front of engine, and line up the holes in both. Then push the gudgeon pin through and fit the second spring clip.

HOW TO RESTORE HONDA FOURS

5.144 Repeat this for all four pistons, ensuring that the arrow mark faces to the front when fitting all. Now fit a new base gasket, O-rings and dowel pins.

5.146 Now put on the head gasket, along with the dowel pins.

5.145 Replacing the cylinder block will be much easier if you can get someone to help you. You need to gently lower the cylinder block over the stud bolts, pass the cam chain through the cylinder block at the same time, while at the same time holding in the piston rings until the pistons slide into the bores. You can use a set of piston ring compressors, but if you lightly oil the pistons and bores, the pistons will slide in quite easily. You must, however, ensure that the rings are compressed enough to allow them to fit inside the bore without catching. If the pistons are not sufficiently compressed they can snap. Do not force down the cylinder: use care and patience when carrying out this step. Working on two pistons at a time, when they are in position, gently tap down the cylinder and start on the next pair of pistons. Once all four pistons are in, tap down the cylinder block until it is set firmly on the crankcase. Fit the cam chain guide now, too.

5.147 Do not forget to replace all rubber gaskets over the dowels that sit at the bottom of the cylinder studs.

THE ENGINE

5.148 Keep the cam chain under light tension at all times to prevent it coming off the crankshaft sprocket and dropping into the crankcase.

5.149 Replace the cylinder head – again, keeping hold of the cam chain. Torque the head nuts to the setting, and in the sequence, given in your workshop manual. Insert all new oil seals and make sure the dowels are in place.

VALVE TIMING AND ADJUSTMENT

All Honda SOHC 4-stroke engines have inlet and exhaust valves that require a mechanism to drive them. The inlet valve opens to allow the fuel/air mixture from the carburettor into the combustion chamber, then closes, and both the inlet and exhaust valves stay closed for the compression stroke. The fuel/air mixture is then compressed by the upward movement of the piston, and at the right time – a fraction before the piston reaches top dead centre – a spark is introduced by the ignition system, igniting the fuel and creating combustion.

Once the engine has fired the piston, it is forced down and the exhaust valve opens to allow exhaust gasses to escape. This happens thousands of times a minute, and is timed very precisely. Each valve has to open an exact amount, and the tappets that operate the valves are adjusted only a few thousandths of an inch. If the valves are adjusted incorrectly, the valve will either open at the wrong time or for the incorrect amount of time, in which case the engine will either run badly or not at all.

The valves are operated by rockers that, in turn, are operated by a camshaft. The camshaft is driven by a cam chain that has a chain tensioner.

The bottom and top ends of the engine have to be timed precisely so that when the piston is at top dead centre (TDC) on the compression stroke, both valves are completely closed. If one is not properly closed there will be no compression and the gasses will not be compressed, giving a misfire or not firing at all. In the worst case scenario the piston could hit a valve, causing major engine damage.

Valves that are old may need to be changed, or at least re-lapped, which is where the face of the valve and the valve seat are polished finely so the valve seats properly and gives a gas-tight seal.

These parts of the cylinder head will need to be set precisely for the engine to run correctly. The camshaft must be set to match the crankshaft so that the cams are in the correct position for each valve relevant to each piston.

67

HOW TO RESTORE HONDA FOURS

5.150 Refit the camshaft carrier, but, before doing so, make sure that the small oilways are 100 per cent clean and clear. It was debris in the camshaft carrier oil passages that caused the camshaft on this engine to overheat and snap.

5.152 To set the valve timing the camshaft should be set to this position. The two machined lines should be level with the join between the carrier and its cap, with the slot to the top.

5.153 Pass the camshaft through the cam chain and onto the carriers. To do this the camshaft sprocket has to be removed from the camshaft. Once the camshaft is on the sprocket, the latter can be pushed back onto the camshaft. Do not bolt on the sprocket yet because it still has to be set in the correct timing position. With the crankshaft and camshaft both set, rotate the sprocket (off the chain) until the two mounting holes line up with those on the camshaft. The camshaft and crankshaft must not move from their positions whilst doing this. Once the sprocket is lined up with the holes in the camshaft, bolt the sprocket to the camshaft.

5.151 Rotate the crankshaft until the T mark for pistons one and four is in-line with the mark above on the crankcase.

THE ENGINE

5.154 Fit all the rocker arms and tighten all camshaft caps.

5.156 On the smaller SOHC Four engines the camshaft caps and rockers are part of the rocker cover. Just fit the camshaft as explained previously, and refit the rocker cover. The valve clearances have to be set through the valve covers.

5.157 Now fit the rocker cover.

5.155 Use a feeler gauge to set the valve clearance correctly.

5.158 Replace the cam chain tensioner and set the tension by loosening the bolt underneath and then locking it with the locknut.

HOW TO RESTORE HONDA FOURS

5.159 Replace the starter motor, making sure that the two threaded holes are to the top. These hold the starter motor cover in place.

5.160a Once the engine is back in the frame, refit the oil filter and top up the oil.

5.160 Refit all side covers: your engine rebuild is complete!

Chapter 6
Brakes, wheels & tyres

When Honda launched the CB750 in 1969 it was the first mass produced motorcycle to be fitted with hydraulic disk brakes as standard. Honda followed this innovative move by fitting all SOHC Fours with hydraulic front disk brakes (twin on the CB750F2/3 and some CB650 models), with a drum brake fitted to the rear. CB750F models also had a rear disk brake.

6.0 A good example of the twin front disk setup on the later 'Comstar' wheel, as fitted to CB750F and CB650 models.

6.1 The typical earlier chrome spoke wheel with a single front disk.

Almost every project bike I have been involved with has had brakes that required restoring. In the past, I have purchased bikes that were apparently almost finished, only to find, on closer inspection, only a single bolt was retaining each calliper on the front brake. Many projects advertised for sale are loosely put together for photographic purposes only, so please take a very close look at all of the brake system components.

I make it a rule now to refurbish all brake components on all my projects as a matter of course. Like carburettor rebuilds, it's not often you can get away with not doing this, and this is one task always on my 'must do' list on every restoration project.

HYDRAULIC DISK BRAKES
Firstly, whilst still fitted to the bike, test the brakes for operation and fluid leaks, and that they're not binding. Check all the hoses and brake lines for splits and cracks, then check the brake pads or shoes for wear. If your Honda has been standing for too long, it's likely the brakes are seized, necessitating a rebuild. In fact, the front callipers on SOHC Fours require regular attention to keep them free, and they will often become tight on a bike that is not regularly used.

On first inspection, if you can achieve some movement with the brake pedal or lever, this is an opportunity to determine if it's possible to free the brake calliper piston (which will help when rebuilding the calliper later, if you need to). Freeing the piston now, before you strip the system, will save time and effort later on trying to remove a seized piston. The pressure from the master cylinder will do all the hard work for you at this stage, and push out the piston (with the caliper removed from the disk).

HOW TO RESTORE HONDA FOURS

6.2 A dangerous brake hose with an obvious split. Carefully check hoses for splits, and seals for leaks.

An hydraulic system that has not been used for a while can suffer from metal corrosion (note that the callipers are alloy and the piston steel), and will be seized. It is also likely that the rubber hoses and seals have perished and will need changing.

The pistons in the master cylinder and the calliper corrode, and the rust makes them stick to the alloy body they are in. If the calliper piston did not move when you first tested it, it will require freeing off before the brakes will work properly.

Rebuilding the brake calliper
This CB750K7 brake calliper is an example of what you're likely to find when restoring the brakes.

A seized piston can be freed in two ways, and the first method, as mentioned earlier, is to operate the brake master cylinder to push out the piston. However, this method will only work if your master cylinder is in good working condition, which, often, they are not.

6.4 A stripped calliper in need of renovation. A new seal will be needed, and the body will benefit from a fresh coat of paint.

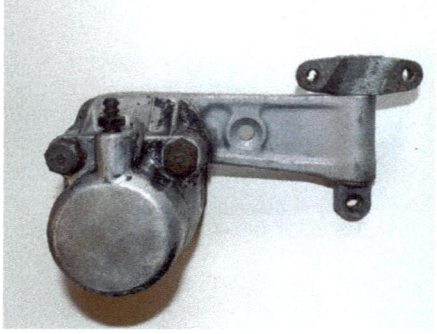

6.3 A typical brake calliper with the mounting bracket.

6.5 The second method is to remove the calliper from the bike. Block the brake hose hole with a suitably-sized bolt, and attach a grease gun to the loosened bleed nipple. The pressure from the grease gun will push out the piston. This method has never failed me. Once the piston is out, the calliper will need thorough cleaning and de-greasing.

BRAKES, WHEELS & TYRES

6.6 Now that the piston is removed from the calliper you'll most likely find that the calliper bore is corroded, and will require thorough cleaning before the piston and new seal can be fitted. Using fine wet and dry paper, remove the corrosion inside the calliper. It must be completely clear of corrosion, and also very smooth. If anything more than a very light sanding is needed the calliper must be renewed or substituted by a refurbished unit.

6.8 Depending on the condition of the paint, you can either give the entire calliper a good rub down with wet and dry abrasive paper until it is smooth, or – if the paint is very bad – use paint stripper to completely remove it. If you do not have spraying equipment, aerosol spray paint will be fine, and on such an exposed part of the bike I would use a harder wearing paint such as Hammerite Smooth. Another advantage of using this type of paint is that priming is not necessary as it is self-priming. If you choose to use cellulose paint make sure the bare metal is primed first. Once the calliper has been de-greased and prepared, you can respray the calliper.

6.7 A corroded piston: the chrome has come off in places. A piston like this must not be reused as it would damage the rubber seal with the danger of brake failure. The rust between the piston and the calliper bore caused this piston to seize.

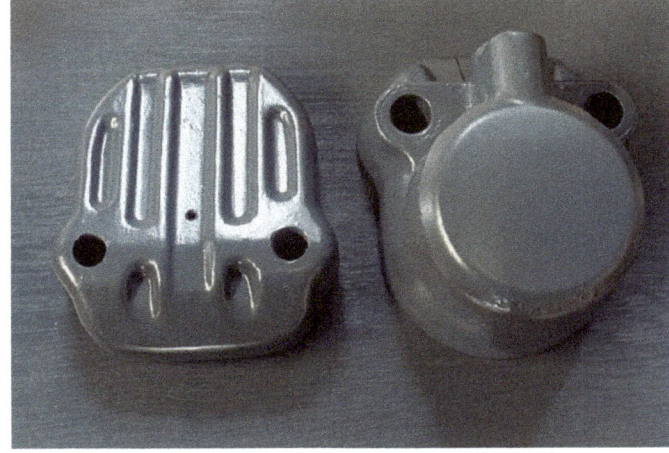

6.9 Unless using an all in-one-paint, apply two coats of primer to the bare calliper. Leave plenty of time for the paint to dry properly before applying the next coat.

HOW TO RESTORE HONDA FOURS

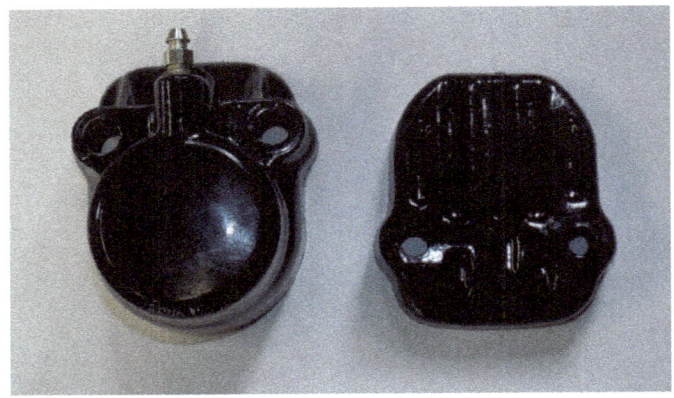

6.10 After two coats of top coat paint the calliper looks like new again, and you can begin to rebuild it. Note new bleed nipple.

6.11 The black rubber seal here will need replacement: carefully prise it out with a small screwdriver or similar.

6.12 This calliper was cleaned in the blast cabinet, and finally polished with 1200 grade wet and dry paper; its now ready for the new piston and seal. Once you have re-sprayed the calliper body fit the new seal.

6.13 New piston and seal ready to be fitted in the calliper.

6.14 Slide the new piston into the calliper. Applying a little brake fluid to the seal will help the piston slide in more easily.

6.15 Always fit new crush washers to the brake hose banjo bolt. These come in either copper or aluminium.

74

BRAKES, WHEELS & TYRES

6.16 I always fit a new brake bleed nipple. Often, the original will break off during removal, so, to avoid this, use the correct size spanner or socket and try to move it a little in each direction. Some nipples will simply not budge, but if you can achieve even a little movement apply, some light oil and it will come out.

6.17 Calliper rebuild complete. Two or three coats of paint make the calliper look like new again.

6.18 The rebuilt calliper refitted to the fork leg.

6.19 The style of calliper fitted to models with a twin front disk arrangement.

6.20 Typical rear drum brake setup as fitted to most SOHC Fours ...

6.21 ... and the rear brake calliper as fitted to all CB750F models.

75

HOW TO RESTORE HONDA FOURS

When the paint has dried and the calliper has been cleaned and polished, it's ready for the new piston and seal kit. Rebuilding the calliper is the reverse of stripping it, but with new seal and piston lubricated with brake fluid before inserting the piston. The refurbished calliper can then be put away, new pads too, until you are ready to refit them to your bike. Note that you can buy stainless steel calliper pistons for most bikes, which is worth considering because these tend not to corrode and seize as easily as the original type of piston. If this option is not viable, apply some copper grease to the piston outside the seal to help prevent it seizing again.

6.22 Brake disks should be checked for cracks. Although I have never come across a disk that wasn't re-usable on a motorcycle, they can become scored, and may require machining or, in extreme cases, renewing. This is not the norm, and most are in usable condition.

Re-building the master cylinder
If the master cylinder is also seized you will need to rebuild it (rebuild kits are available for all models). Try to operate the brake lever: if it moves, it's unlikely that the master cylinder is seized, although it's worth considering a precautionary rebuild if it did not produce sufficient fluid pressure to move a seized calliper piston.

Carefully begin to strip the master cylinder. The following is the most common procedure.

Once the cylinder has been cleaned thoroughly, fit the new piston and seal kit. Insert the new piston with seals into the master cylinder after lubricating them with brake fluid. Then sit the new circlip on top of the piston and, with your circlip pliers squeeze

6.23 Start by draining all fluid from the reservoir into a suitable container (discard in the correct manner). Remove the master cylinder from the handlebars by unscrewing the two bolts. Protect the paintwork from brake fluid splashes, as this will damage paint and decals.

6.24 The brake hoses are likely to need renewing, though store them safely if they really are in good condition. Unscrew the brake hose banjo bolt (there will be a small amount of brake fluid when you undo the bolt so have a cloth ready).

BRAKES, WHEELS & TYRES

6.25 With the cylinder on the bench, remove the brake lever by undoing the small nut and bolt and removing the cap. Note that the hose bolt has been replaced for safekeeping.

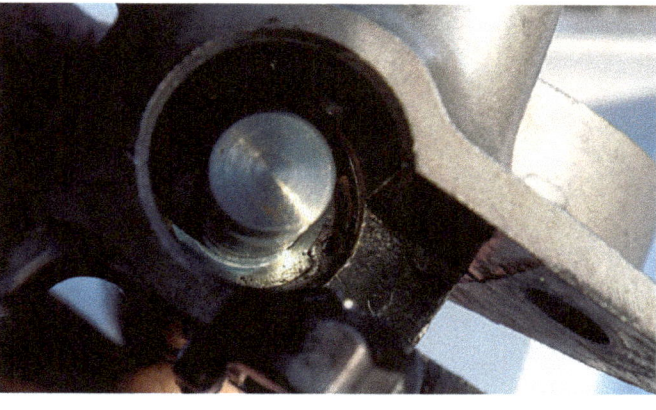

6.28 Inside the body of the master cylinder, where the brake lever pushes onto the piston, a spring clip retains the dust boot. Remove the spring clip and pull out the rubber dust cover (this usually splits and is no longer usable). The dust cover on this master cylinder was already missing. Underneath you will see a circlip.

6.26 Remove the cap. Check inside the fluid reservoir and clean as much as you can with a cloth to see if you can find the holes at the bottom of the reservoir. The inside of the reservoir is usually dirty, and the two holes blocked. The holes should be free from debris to allow fluid to pass through, so clean thoroughly.

6.29 Use long-nose circlip pliers to remove the circlip (this can be a little awkward). I have found that, sometimes, the points of the circlip pliers are too large to fit into the circlip holes, in which case I have had to grind or file the points to make them slimmer.

6.27 This master cylinder has been cleaned: the two holes are showing and it's ready for rebuilding.

6.30 Now the piston can be pulled from the master cylinder. The cylinder will require cleaning and de-greasing, ready for the new piston kit.

HOW TO RESTORE HONDA FOURS

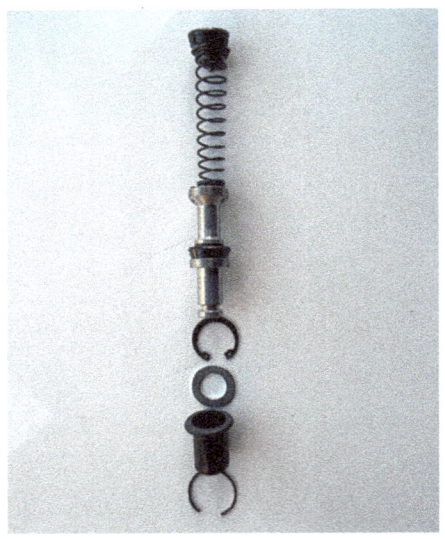

6.31 The new master cylinder piston and seal assembly ready to be fitted.

6.32 Now completely clean and de-greased, ready to fit the piston seal kit.

6.33 The inside of this brake drum always has a light layer of rust, which should be cleaned off.

6.34 Using some 240 wet and dry paper, sand the drum back to a clean metal surface.

the circlip just enough for it to slip into the master cylinder bore, and then release so that it sits inside the circlip groove. It is important to check that the circlip has actually gone into the slot properly. If it hasn't, the piston will pop back out again.

Fit the new dust cover and spring clip to hold it in. The master cylinder is now re-built.

DRUM BRAKES

Drum brakes are less of a problem to restore than hydraulic disk brakes, and generally require only stripping, cleaning and reassembling with new brake shoes.

Cables

Check all break cables for correct routing. A cable may have been put on quickly for a photo or to make the bike look more complete, and could be routed incorrectly: this could tighten

BRAKES, WHEELS & TYRES

6.35 After a few minutes' work the brake drum is clean and ready for the brake hub.

6.38 Although I always recommend fitting new brake shoes if existing ones have only a light glaze, it is possible to give them a light rub down with some wet and dry paper, which will remove scoring and glaze. Wear a dust mask to do this because some brake material contains asbestos, and is dangerous if inhaled. (This should only be carried out if the brake shoe is not worn below the recommended wear limit.)

6.36 The brake shoes here are showing signs of scoring, and are lightly glazed.

6.39 To remove the shoes pull out the two split pins ...

6.37 Check that the brake shoes are not badly worn: these are showing little wear and are still usable.

6.40 ... lift off the anchor pin washer ...

HOW TO RESTORE HONDA FOURS

6.41 ... remove the two springs with a pair of pliers, and the shoes can be lifted out.

6.42 The new brake shoes ready to be fitted.

6.43 Use some Plasticine to make a funnel around a cable and add light oil to it. Overnight, the oil will make its way down the entire length of the cable (this method will work on lightly corroded cables). I have had cables that are so corroded they have snapped under light pressure. If in any doubt about your bike's cables, change them: you don't want to be miles from home when a cable breaks.

when the handlebars are turned which would affect the throttle and possibly catch out a rider. This has happened to me in the past. Check for frayed cables, which, if they will not return correctly, could result in a sticky clutch or throttle.

Oiling cables

This method has been used for years and still works well today; it can be used on all of the cables on your bike.

Find somewhere quite high to hang the cable vertically, so that it does not touch the ground. Use a piece of plasticine to make a small funnel that is sealed to the cable outer casing. Hang the cable up and pour a small amount of light oil into the funnel (ensure the cable is suspended over a suitable container to catch the oil). After 24 hours, check if the cable will begin to move. If stuck firm, buy a new cable.

WHEELS

Other than the later model which used Comstar wheels, all Honda SOHC models use plain steel, chrome-plated rims with spokes.

Often, wheels are in poor condition: check they're not buckled or damaged in any way; and check all spokes for tightness. If you have aftermarket alloy wheels fitted, check for hairline cracks and chips in the alloy.

If you're lucky, a good clean and polish will restore the wheels to like new condition; if unlucky, the wheels may need rebuilding, and it can be cheaper to look around for a good used replacement, rather than having a wheel rebuilt.

If the chrome plating on your wheels is in very poor condition or the wheels are damaged, new wheel rims can be bought, in which case, the wheels will need to be stripped down and completely rebuilt. The spokes are taken out and the hubs checked over before the wheels are re-assembled. Wheel rebuilding is a specialist job not suitable for an amateur to undertake.

However, other jobs – better suited to an amateur – will improve overall appearance of your wheels.

For example, brake disks often have a painted centre; the disks can be re-painted, making a whole lot of difference to the finished look of your motorcycle.

Start by removing the spindle and taking off the wheel; then remove the disks as shown. You will need to tap back the locking tabs before you can undo the disk bolts.

De-grease the disk and dry it thoroughly. Tape areas that are not going to be painted. Some difficult to tape areas could be sprayed, but you

6.44 If the brake disk needs painting, remove it in order to spray both sides easily. Tap back the locking tabs to enable the brake disk retaining nuts to be undone.

BRAKES, WHEELS & TYRES

6.45 Remove all retaining nuts so the disk can be pulled away from the wheel.

6.46 Turn over the wheel and tap the disk from behind to loosen it.

6.48 Use a small paintbrush for the difficult-to-reach areas.

will need to remove the paint on these areas later on.

The hubs can be difficult to polish properly: use a small multi-tool with a polishing head to get into the hard-to-reach areas.

6.47 Use masking tape to mask areas that are not going to be painted.

6.49 The wheel with disks removed: now is the time to polish the hub.

81

HOW TO RESTORE HONDA FOURS

6.50 Light alloy corrosion is easily polished out.

6.52 After a short while we have a nicely polished hub.

6.51 Polishing the difficult areas with a multi-tool.

6.53 Check the cush drive rubbers for deterioration, and examine both front and rear wheel bearings for wear.

BRAKES, WHEELS & TYRES

TYRES

Tyre condition is essential to roadworthiness. Perishing, insufficient tread, splits and cuts affect safety and, if present, a new tyre is required. You should renew any tyre known to be five or more years old, regardless of appearance.

I have never had a restoration project where the tyres were in good enough condition to re-use. Always allow for a new set of tyres in your project, and don't forget to include the inner tubes and rim tape, too.

Never combine old and new tyres.

6.54 A tyre clearly marked for rear use, and showing rotation arrow.

All new tyres are marked as 'Front' and 'Rear,' which may sound obvious but sometimes can be overlooked.

Tyres should be changed in pairs and be from the same manufacturer. The tyres are designed to work together and as a pair to maintain optimum handling performance. The manufacturer of your motorcycle will recommend a tyre type and make, and there's likely to be a modern-day equivalent for your bike if the original is no longer available.

Always fit new inner tubes with

6.55 A tyre showing clear signs of perishing. Dangerous and illegal: if your tyre is worn or looks like this, renewal is the only option.

new tyres. An old inner tube will be stretched, and can crease and fail due to the thin rubber.

Many tyre manufacturers still make tyres for classic motorcycles. These retain the classic look, although many riders fit more modern tyres because they often give better grip and more confident riding experience than the older type of tyre.

6.56 After twenty years on the wheel, removing this tyre was a two-man job.

It's possible to change or fit tyres yourself using tyre levers, but if your project has been unused for some time you will find that the rubber has gone very hard, making it almost impossible to remove. If you take your wheels to the motorcycle shop where you are buying your tyres they will fit the tyres for free. This is the best option, with the added benefit that the wheels will be balanced at the same time – something you can't do at home

With the old tyre removed, it's very likely that the inside of the rim (under the inner tube) will have some rust, which the tyre fitter will remove with a wire brush, and then fit rim tape to cover the heads of the spokes, Should any rust reappear, it will not affect the tyre by causing a puncture because the rim tape will cover it.

Here, the fitter is about to fit the

6.57 Wheel tightly clamped and new rim tape fitted; the tape prevents the spoke heads from touching the inner tube.

HOW TO RESTORE HONDA FOURS

new Bridgestone tyre to the wheel. With the wheel tightly clamped to the machine, the tyre is easier to fit.

6.58 Make sure the fitter knows the direction of rotation of the wheel, which is not obvious, and should be pointed out prior to fitment of the new tyre.

Check what the correct tyre pressures are for your motorcycle, information which will be found in the user's handbook or in a workshop manual. Ensuring correct tyre inflation is the most important tyre maintenance you can perform, as correct tyre pressure will improve safety on the road.

Under-inflated tyres can result in imprecise cornering, higher running temperatures and overheating, irregular tread wear at the edge of the contact patch, and eventual failure.

Over inflation will result in a hard ride and accelerated tyre wear in the centre of the contact patch.

Check cold tyre pressure frequently with a good quality gauge, especially before long-distance trips.

6.59 Lastly, the essential tyre pressure check. It is important to have correct tyre pressures or safety issues and early wear problems can result.

6.60 Time to go now – other customers are waiting.

BRAKES, WHEELS & TYRES

6.61 The finished wheel and tyre combination, cleaned, repainted, and with new rubber. Be aware that the tyres will require approximately 100km or 60 miles 'scrubbing in' before they reach optimum performance.

Chapter 7
Fuel & exhaust systems

All Honda SOHC Fours are equipped with four carburettors, which should be adjusted and synchronised correctly to ensure the smooth running of the engine. If your Honda has not been run for a considerable period of time, it's likely that the entire fuel system will be contaminated with stale fuel, dirt and scale. The carburettors and fuel tap are probably seized; fuel pipes will have gone hard and brittle, and the air filter could be completely blocked. The entire system will require cleaning and rebuilding before being reinstalled on your project bike.

Initially, whilst stripping the bike down to basic components, we had a quick look to assess the state of the fuel system components. Now it's time to take a closer look at the fuel and exhaust systems, because faults in these will result in poor running, or not running at all.

THE FUEL TANK

It is of paramount importance to ensure that any rust or scale is completely removed from the fuel tank: even small particles will cause running problems by blocking the filters in the fuel tap, or the carburettors.

Rust remover can be used effectively on the inside of the fuel tank, followed by a resin fuel tank liner if thought necessary.

Fuel tanks often contain rust, scale, or even old fuel that has turned to sludge at the bottom of the tank. All must be thoroughly cleaned out before refuelling.

If the tank is more seriously

7.0 If the inside of your tank looks like this, it will require attention before you can put in fuel.

7.1 This tank shows only slight surface rust and will require only a light clean. Rinse out the tank with a small amount of two stroke oil/petrol mix. Swill around so that the fuel reaches all corners of the tank, then empty into a suitable container. This process will swill out any small particles; the addition of a small amount of two stroke oil in the fuel will help prevent further rust forming.

contaminated, further cleaning will be necessary. Begin by removing the fuel tap and set it aside for a closer inspection later. Various methods exist for cleaning the inside of the tank. If your tank has sludge and scale, one way is to place a few handfuls of small gravel (such as that used in aquariums) in the tank and shake: this

FUEL & EXHAUST SYSTEMS

helps abrade the inside of the tank and loosen encrusted debris.

Find some way of blocking the fuel tap hole – a piece of cork from a wine bottle does the job – to prevent washing and rust-removing fluid leaking out. Then, rinse the tank with a warm, soapy water solution. Empty the water and dry; follow with the rust remover solution.

7.2 When the rust-removing process is complete, dry the tank thoroughly. I place my tank on a small, oil-filled radiator on a very low heat setting for a few hours to make sure the tank is 100 per cent dry inside. You can also use a hairdryer to blow warm air into and through the tank. Whichever method you use, the tank needs to be completely dry to avoid any further rust build-up.

If your tank is in particularly bad condition you could consider lining it with a resin-based tank sealer, which will also bind together any rust or scale that could not be removed and fill any tiny pinholes there may be.

Finally, carry out any cosmetic work to your tank – for further details refer to the chapter on spraying.

If the tank condition is not too bad, add (once the fuel tap is refitted) some fuel with a small amount of two stroke oil. Give this a light swill round and the oil will coat the sides of the tank and prevent rust reforming. A little two-stroke oil in the fuel will not harm a four-stroke engine, as it will burn off a small amount quickly, though may smoke more when running. This is a fuel tank storage precaution, and should not be employed on a day-to-day basis, when neat fuel should be used.

Now set aside the tank until later.

Fuel tap

Dismantle the fuel tap, being careful not to lose any small parts such as springs, screws, etc.

When dismantling the fuel tap or carburettor, try not to tear the gaskets or seals. Although it is recommended that all seals and gaskets are replaced, as it may prove difficult to source some, you may be able to re-use one or two, or use them as patterns.

The fuel taps and carburettor fittings can often be seized solid, and some gentle persuasion will be necessary to release them. Cover with light oil and let it soak for a while to penetrate the threads and joints before attempting to move them.

7.3 Some fuel taps are held on by a large nut, while others are held on by two screws.

7.4 Unscrew the fuel tap from the tank and store the screws safely. Any sealing washers should be renewed. There will be at least one O-ring or other rubber seal between the fuel tap and the tank, which will also need renewal.

HOW TO RESTORE HONDA FOURS

7.5 Once the fuel tap is off, place it on a clean surface ready for dismantling. This tap from a CB750 is a sealed unit and not serviceable: however, other taps can be dismantled for cleaning and replacement of seals, etc. A small amount of fuel will probably spill when you remove the bowl, so have some cloth ready to catch this.

7.6 Unscrew the fuel tap bowl. Be prepared for some fuel to spill out.

7.7 It is usual to find some particles of rust and scale in the bowl. Note the condition of the rubber seal and save if not damaged.

7.8 Once the bowl is removed you will see the fuel tap filter. Gently remove and clean with carburettor cleaner, then blow through with an airline.

7.9 Next, remove the tap arm by unscrewing the faceplate screws.

FUEL & EXHAUST SYSTEMS

7.10 Once the tap is off you can see the rubber seal. Gently lift this out using a small screwdriver, trying not to split the seal (it may come in useful later). Often, the fuel tap is completely blocked, as can be seen in this photo.

7.11 Now, only the fuel tap body remains. Once dismantled, you will be able to see the passages that the fuel flows through. Every passageway should be cleaned thoroughly. Using an airline, try to blow through the passages. If they are completely blocked, using a small, pointed object – such as a watchmaker's-type screwdriver – to gently dig out the scale and push through the passages. Use carburettor cleaner when the passages are virtually clear to remove any varnish deposits.

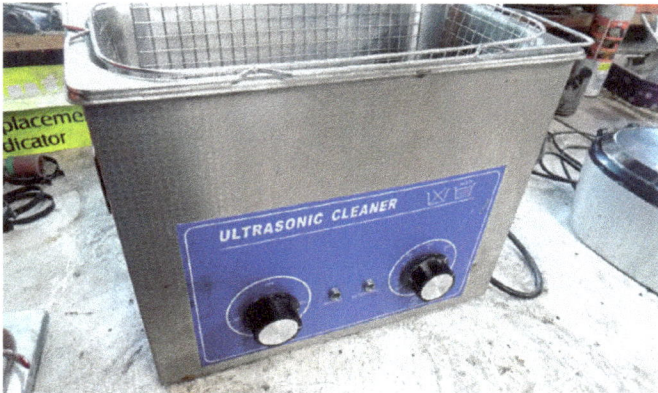

7.12 and 7.13 Ideally, an ultrasonic cleaner should be employed at this point (small examples are inexpensive, and suitable for use on smaller items). When cleaning larger items, such as the carburettor body, a larger model will be necessary, but if you don't have an ultrasonic cleaner, use carburettor cleaner and a small pointed object.

If the seals and gaskets came out in one piece it may be possible to reuse them, although it's always best to fit a rebuild kit if you can find one.

7.14 When everything is cleaned, rebuild the fuel tap (reverse order of disassembly). Once fitted, the fuel tap should work like new again.

HOW TO RESTORE HONDA FOURS

THE CARBURETTOR
This section shows the strip down and rebuild of the carburettors. Carburettor components on the CB750 are similar to those on other Honda Four models, with only minor differences between them. Your workshop manual will provide more detail about your specific carburettor.

When dismantling the carbs, it's a good idea to make notes and take photos to remind you where the parts go when you rebuild them.

The main objective of cleaning carburettors is to ensure that all air passages are completely clean and free from obstruction, as they tend to become clogged whilst in use. On all projects I recommend a full strip down and rebuild of the carburettors unless your bike was running flawlessly when you bought it.

7.17 Check the rubbers once they are off: sometimes they are split and need to be replaced.

7.15 Disconnect all cables and fuel pipes, leaving only the carburettors and rubbers in place. Carburettor to cylinder connections vary, in that some are rubber; some are a rubber-alloy combination. If your bike has rubber connections, check for splits or perishing, in which case they will need to be renewed.

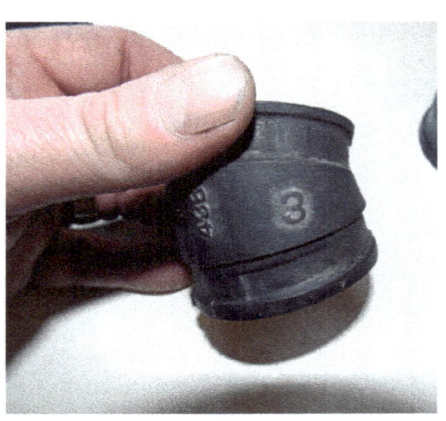

7.18 On some models Honda numbered the rubbers for each cylinder. On other models you'll need to mark them to know which cylinder to replace them on.

7.16 This rubber manifold is from a CB750, which has a rubber-only connection between carburettor and cylinder. Over the years, the rubbers will often have gone very hard, and become more like plastic. Loosen the clamps holding the rubbers and then prise off the rubbers and carburettors from the engine block.

7.19 On other Honda Four(s) alloy-rubber combinations are used. In this instance, be very careful when trying to remove the carburettors on a motorcycle that has not been used for years, as the rubber can break away from the alloy, making the small manifold unusable. This is an example of a damaged rubber. This type uses a rubber O-ring seal which must be replaced with a new one.

FUEL & EXHAUST SYSTEMS

7.20 The carburettors are all connected to an alloy mounting block. Each carb is held on by two crosshead screws, as shown here.

7.23 The CB750 has a rubber boot that covers the pivot arm on top of the carburettor. On other models the carburettor slide has an alloy cover that should be removed.

7.21 To separate the carburettors for cleaning, remove all screws.

7.24 Once the mounting block has been removed, it is easier to access the other split pins. Then, it's simply a case of pulling the carburettors from the fuel hoses that connect them.

7.22 The carburettors also have interconnecting rods, attached by a tiny split pin. Close this and remove it, trying not to lose it or the washer that accompanies it.

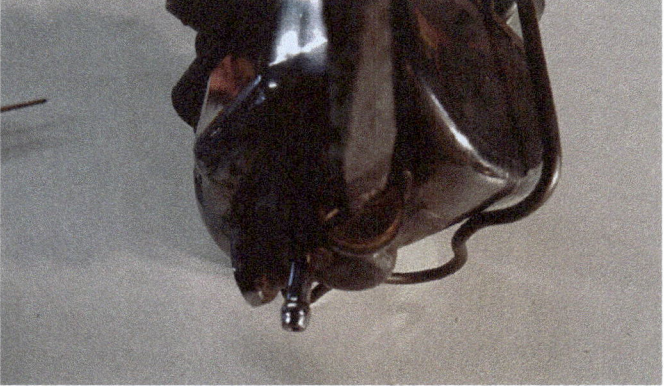

7.25 Any fuel left in the carburettor bowl should be drained. On most carburettors there's a brass drain screw or bolt at the bottom of the bowl. Unscrew this over a container to catch the fuel.

HOW TO RESTORE HONDA FOURS

7.26 If you do not have a drain screw on your carburettor bowl, place the overflow pipes in a suitable jar and tip the carburettor until the fuel drains out.

7.27 Now the carburettors are separated into individual units we can begin to strip them for inspection. Unscrew the knurled top ...

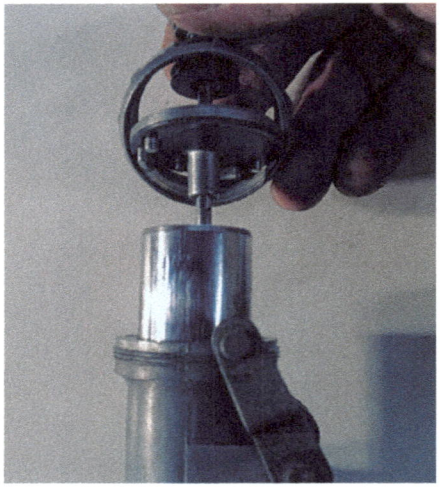

7.28 ... and pull out the carburettor slide.

7.29 Note the slot in the carburettor slide ...

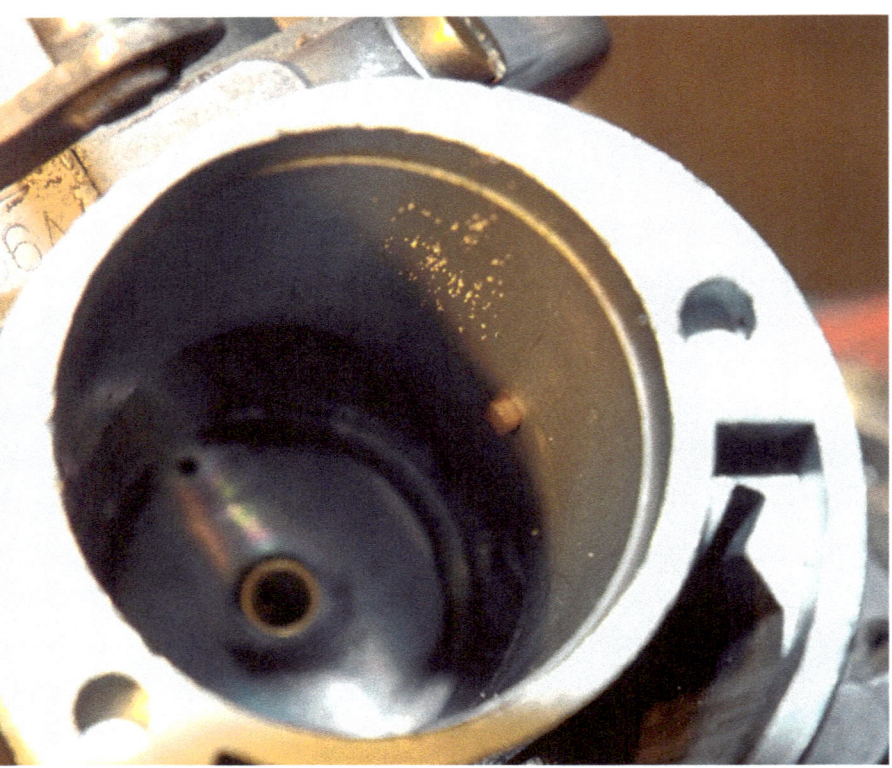

7.30 ... which locates over a peg inside the carburettor body to ensure the slide is fitted facing the correct direction.

FUEL & EXHAUST SYSTEMS

Once removed, prepare a very clean work area on which to begin dismantling the carburettors.

TIP! Find a small, clean, plastic container (margarine tub) for each carburettor and, when dismantling, place all the pieces of individual carburettor in individual containers.

Clean the main body of each carb to remove any dirt and grime before dismantling: this will help prevent contamination of internal parts when dismantling. Dismantle one carburettor at a time, ensuring all its parts are contained in one container.

7.32 Once the bowl is off take a look inside – we can see that this example needs a good clean. The float and jets are now visible.

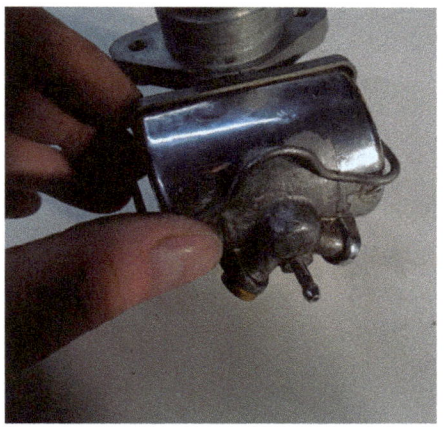

7.31 Push up the float chamber retaining clip. On most models the float bowl will be held on by four crosshead screws: remove these and set aside; try not to damage the bowl gasket. Any fuel that is left will run out so have your container ready. Remember: NO NAKED FLAMES!

7.33 Remove the metal float pin by using a small, pointed object to push it out.

HOW TO RESTORE HONDA FOURS

7.34 The pins usually push out quite easily, but if they don't lightly tap the pointed object with a hammer to help move the pin.

7.37 The jets are removed by using an 8mm spanner and flat blade screwdriver. The float valve will require a socket to remove. Replace the fibre washer if it looks damaged.

7.35 Once the float is removed check for pinholes by submerging in warm water. If you see bubbles, this means there are holes, and the float will have to be replaced. A brass float that has holes can be repaired with a small spot of solder.

7.38 Thoroughly clean all jets. Note the filter on the float valve.

7.36 Inside the carburettor we can see the slow jet (right), main jet (centre), the float valve (left), and seat.

7.39 This close-up shows the amount of scale that has built up, with some holes completely blocked.

FUEL & EXHAUST SYSTEMS

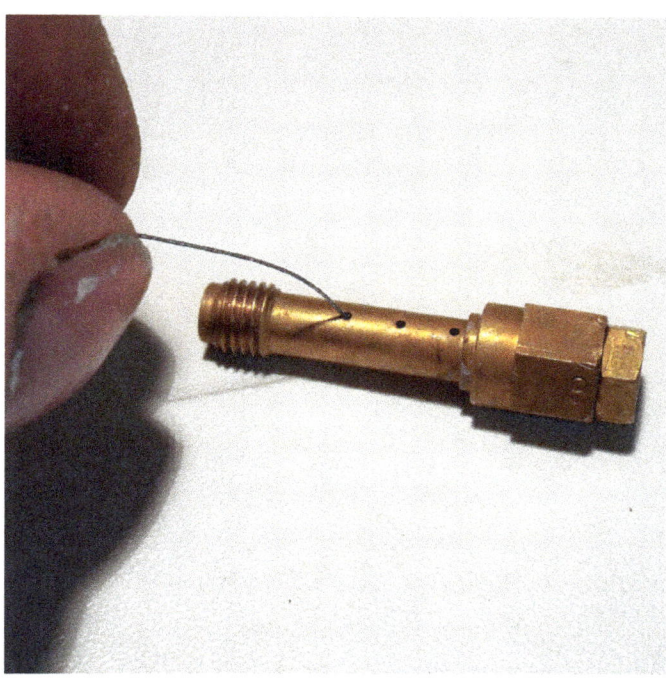

7.40 Any particles that are firmly stuck will have to be pushed out with a piece of wire. Also flush with carburettor cleaner to remove any fine deposits.

7.42 Now, with only the main carburettor body remaining, thoroughly clean inside and out before rebuilding the carburettor.

7.41 Remove the air screw and vacuum gauge attachment screw, and clean with carburettor cleaner, but before removing the air screw, screw it in with a screwdriver, noting the number of turns. When replacing the air screw, screw fully in and turn out the same number of turns, to achieve a basic fuel/air mixture setting when rebuilding the carburettor.

7.43 Rebuild the components in the reverse order you dismantled them, using fully cleaned or new parts.

HOW TO RESTORE HONDA FOURS

7.44 Replace the float, insert the pin and refit the float bowl.

7.45 Fit new connecting hose and ensure the fuel union is inserted in both carburettors (do this with both pairs).

7.46 Don't forget to refit the spring connector between the centre two carbs.

7.47 Replace all connecting rods.

7.48 Refit the back plate.

FUEL & EXHAUST SYSTEMS

7.49 Replace all washers and split pins.

7.50 Ensure that the fork arms are correctly fitted, as shown, before screwing on the back plate.

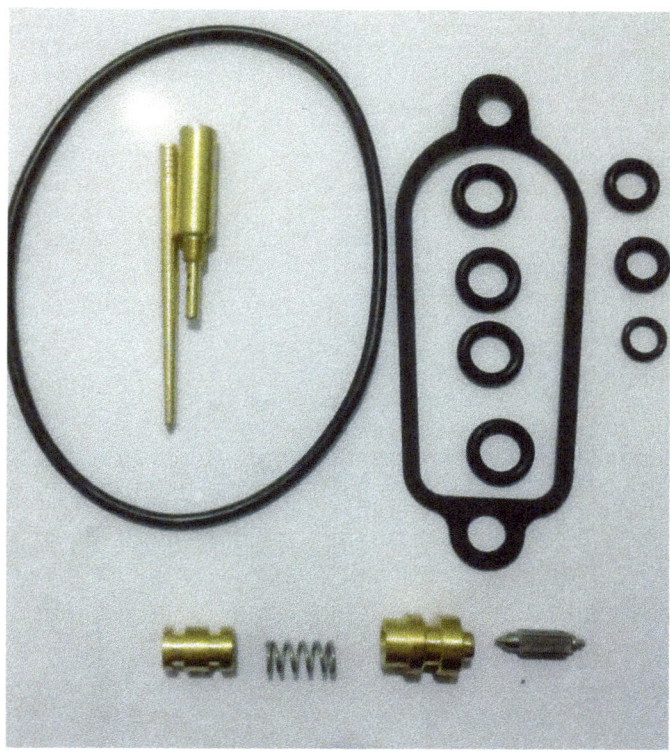

7.51 I recommend that a carburettor rebuild kit be fitted; a genuine one if possible, although aftermarket kits are usually okay. This is a rebuild kit from a 1976 Honda CB400 Four Super Sport.

7.52 A set of carburettors from a 1977 CB750K7 with new fuel pipes fitted. You can see the accelerator pump housing on carburettor number two.

Once the carbs are rebuilt, set the float height and jets according to your workshop manual. Now put the carbs in a clean container out of the way so no dust can contaminate them, ready to go back on your bike's engine. Once they are refitted to the engine they will require balancing so that they are synchronised with each other.

HOW TO RESTORE HONDA FOURS

THE EXHAUST SYSTEM

An exhaust system in good condition on a classic Honda Four is a big asset, as most are in poor condition, with rusty holes, dents, or scratched chrome. The exhaust system is also one of the most difficult secondhand parts to source in good condition. Some aftermarket replicas are very good, but can be expensive.

There are many aftermarket options that do not replicate the original exhaust, and these are offered at a much lower price than the replica systems. If you do buy an aftermarket exhaust, be sure it is intended for road use: many exhausts are for racetrack use only, and are not legal to use on public roads.

The exhaust system has no serviceable parts. Other than keeping the exhaust clean and making sure the exhaust joints and gaskets do not let gasses escape there is little to do. Acid in the exhaust fumes can cause silencers to develop holes, and will require a braze repair if a replacement is not available. Check for cracks and holes in the exhaust system: a cause of failure in a roadworthiness test. Check all joints for exhaust gas leaks. Gaskets and exhaust seals are normally available for joints and connecting to the cylinder head. Where possible, renew any seals between joints.

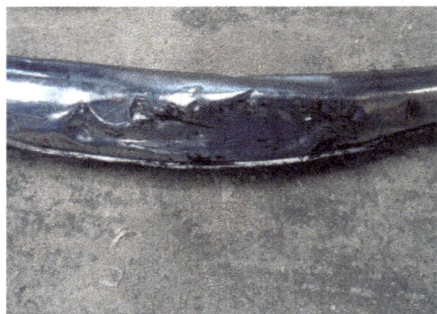

7.53 Damage caused by over-enthusiastic cornering or an accident is often seen on the exhaust system. This is not repairable. If the damage is on the underside and has not caused a split or a hole, you could consider reusing the exhaust as such damage will not affect performance.

7.55 The exhaust seal in the cylinder head is usually a large, crush-type washer, made of copper or aluminium, which should be renewed and not reused.

7.54 An example of an aftermarket exhaust for a CB750K7. Note that this is a 4-into-1 system which was not the original layout for a K7. This was obtained at a motorcycle auto jumble swap meeting for a very reasonable price, and would make a suitable replacement if the original system is not available.

7.56 With good condition, original exhaust systems hard to find, an alternative may be the only option. These exhaust silencers are not original Honda and, in fact, are from a 500 Benelli. Nevertheless, they look great on this Honda, and still retain the 4-into-4 style that this motorcycle originally had.

FUEL & EXHAUST SYSTEMS

7.57 Earlier models all had 4-into-4 exhaust systems, as shown here on this CB750K2.

7.58 Later F models had a sporty 4-into-1 system, as shown on this CB750F1.

Chapter 8
Electrics

The Honda SOHC Four's electrical system was very reliable and of good quality when new, but poor maintenance and time take a toll on wiring, and the electrical system will require a thorough check to reduce the risk of future problems.

Many running problems are electric-related, and many older motorcycles will have suffered from poor wiring repairs. If multiple repairs have been carried out, it's often easiest simply to replace the entire loom. Aftermarket wiring harnesses are available, and could prove a wise investment.

Most electrical problems can be resolved simply by replacing the faulty part. Sparkplugs, points, and starter solenoids are all low-cost components that are not serviceable. Those parts that are serviceable are more likely to be bigger items, such as the starter motor, the price of which is much higher, making it more cost-effective to repair.

FAULTS AND PRECAUTIONS

When removing electrical components, be very careful with the connectors, and, as mentioned before, always pull the connectors, not the wires. This way, the wires will not be pulled from the connector terminal.

There are three reasons why electrics can fail –
• Open circuit faults: a wire has broken or become detached, causing a break in the electrical circuit
• Short circuit faults: cuts/breaks in the wire cause the live wire to touch part of the frame, or other metal items.
• Grounded circuit fault: power is shorted to ground before the switch, resulting in lack of control over power. This is often demonstrated by a light that should not be on, but is.

Some electrical faults will cause a fuse to blow and, until the fault is found and rectified, the fuse will continue to blow.

The most common reason for a fuse blowing is a short circuit: insulation around the wire becomes worn or trapped, exposing the copper, causing a short or component failure. However, even a bulb blowing can trigger a blown fuse.

Beneath the fuel tank, the seat, or even inside the headlamp shell are all places where a wire can become trapped, break down and short circuit.

Wires can also become worn by constant abrasion in areas where there are moving parts, so check especially around handlebars, wheels and the chain, where a wire might not be correctly routed.

When removing parts, pull apart the connectors one by one to check them. Once a connector is apart, clean the terminals with a little wet and dry paper until shiny. Most connectors will have a patina coating that has built up over the years and results in a bad connection. If you clean the terminal when removing or replacing a part, by the end of your project all connectors will have been done and there shouldn't be any future problems.

Ensure the push fit connectors fit firmly: many become loose over time, and need to be squeezed tightly so that they fit snugly again. The same applies to fuse holders; often, these are either dirty or do not hold the fuse tightly enough.

Check the wiring for bad repairs such as poorly crimped connectors, incorrectly fitted Scotchlocks, and joints that are only held together with insulating tape (repairs covered with insulating tape should have the tape removed to check quality and effectiveness of repair).

Two tools can help diagnose almost any electrical problem: a multi-meter and a test light. A test light is

ELECTRICS

nothing more than a 12 volt light with a positive and negative lead, that quickly and easily checks for power in a circuit: no power, no light – simple. Great for checking for breaks in wires.

The multi-meter can do this, but also has numerous other functions: it can check continuity, measure resistance and amperage, and check for bad grounds.

motorcycle batteries are now sealed, maintenance-free units. The following are a few simple preventative measures to keep your battery working well for a long time.

Invest in a decent battery optimiser-type charger! These are not expensive, and will monitor battery condition and charge as needed while the battery is stored. If you intend to store your bike for more than a month, remove the battery and connect to a charger such as this. For winter storage, remove the battery and place in a cool, dry area, charging it once a month at least.

Avoid leaving your motorcycle running at idle for long periods as charging systems generally aren't capable of sufficient output at idle to charge the battery, and run the bike at the same time, slowly draining the battery as a result.

8.1 Multi-meters are inexpensive, and invaluable when working on electrics. As with any piece of equipment, read the instructions that come with the multi-meter before attempting to use it.

8.2 A modern, sealed 12v gel battery: low maintenance and does not need to be topped up with de-ionised water like older batteries.

WIRING DIAGRAMS

When it comes to troubleshooting electrical problems, the most useful tool you can have is a proper electrical wiring diagram of your motorcycle, usually found in a workshop manual, although there are some good colour wiring diagrams available to download free on various internet websites. I have even seen an interactive version.

Learn to interpret this, become familiar with it, and time spent hunting down electrical problems will be much reduced.

Remember: an uninsulated live wire can cause a fire!

When it comes to electrical repairs, along with your basic bike tool kit, I recommend the following –
- Insulating tape
- Spare bulbs (in bubble wrap to protect them)
- Combination wire cutters/strippers/crimpers
- An assorted selection of solderless crimp connectors
- Spare fuses
- Small cable ties (also known as tie wraps)
- 12VDC test light
- A copy of your bike's wiring diagram

THE BATTERY

The battery is the heart of a motorcycle's electrical system, and not only stores and releases electricity as needed, but plays an important role as a 'shock absorber' for voltage spikes and current surges. Properly maintained, a good quality battery will provide years of service.

The vast majority of modern

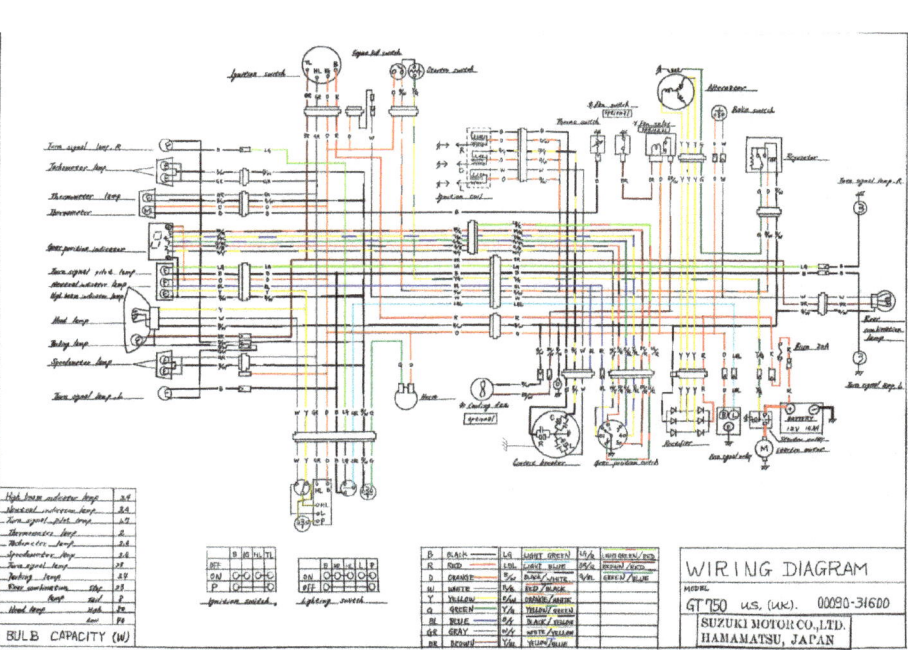

8.3 A typical colour-coded wiring diagram. (Courtesy Suzuki)

HOW TO RESTORE HONDA FOURS

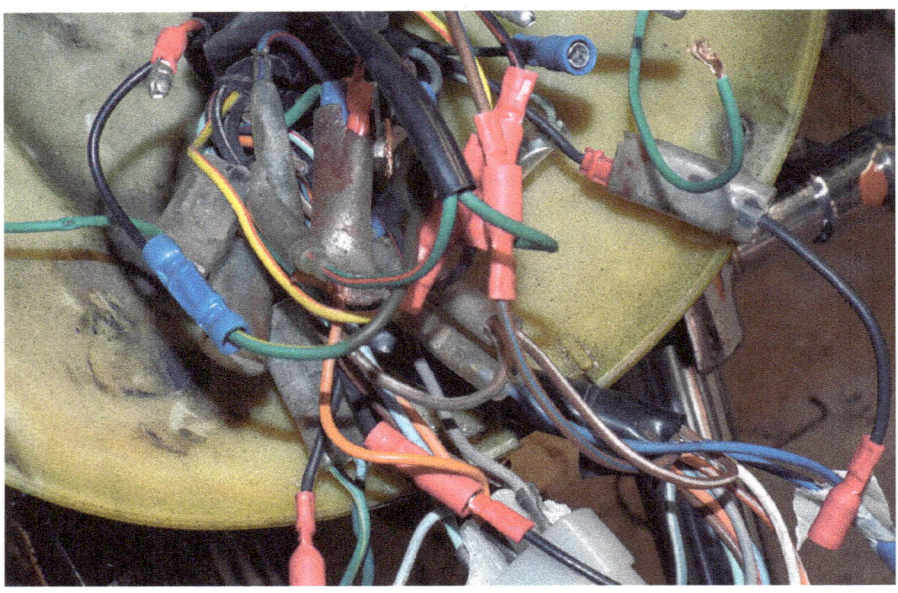

8.4 What a mess! Poor wiring with makeshift repairs will give you endless problems.

8.6 Clean the terminals inside all bulb holders, and check all earth connections.

Generally. I like to keep the cost of restorations to a reasonable level, but sometimes overall condition of the wiring is so bad that it warrants investment in a complete new loom. If you find there's not one available for your bike (at the time of writing these were available for all SOHC Fours from aftermarket suppliers), there are places that will make them for you. Often, looms are comprised of sub-sections, and you may need only one section. You could also opt for a completely new wiring loom rebuild: providing you have a wiring diagram, a knowledgeable car/bike electrician can do this.

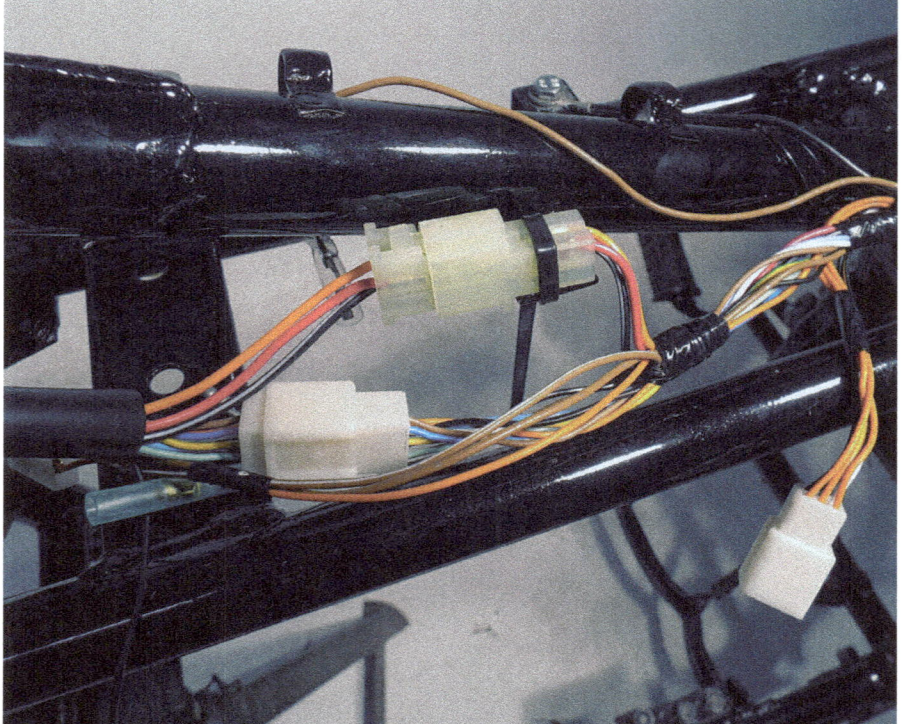

8.7 This bulb holder also doubled-up as a homemade test lamp – ideal when checking for basic connection faults, or manually setting the contact breaker points on the ignition.

8.5 This is what the wiring should look like once fitted: well spread out with nice clean connectors, and no broken wires.

ELECTRICS

8.8 The most common fault on electrical circuits is a bad earth, particularly if the frame has just been sprayed or powder-coated. Remove the earth leads, clean with wet and dry paper until bright, and also clean paint from the frame to which the earth lead bolts. This will give a solid earth connection.

8.9 Remember, before you spend hours troubleshooting the electrics, check the fusebox, as a blown or missing fuse could be the reason. Keep some spare fuses in your bike's side panel or under the seat.

IGNITION AND CHARGING SYSTEMS

The ignition and charging systems are elements of the electrical system. On the ignition side, the Honda SOHC Fours have a battery, ignition coil, contact breaker points, and condensers, finishing with the sparkplug, although some later models do have electronic ignition, which requires little or no maintenance, other than ensuring that the ignition timing is accurately set. Thankfully, all of these parts are replaceable, and generally reasonably priced.

8.10 The contact breaker points, or just 'points,' as they are commonly known, are the most common cause of ignition problems on classic motorcycles. If the gap that the points are set to open at is not correct, the engine will not run, or will run poorly, so at the very least clean the points and check the gap (set according to the workshop manual).

8.11 Check if the points are pitted, which happens when the spark that jumps across the gap causes the surface of the points to erode (pit), as in the picture. These points cannot be set correctly: renewal is the only option.

HOW TO RESTORE HONDA FOURS

Points are a very important part of the ignition system, and inexpensive to buy, so always fit a new set. Very good aftermarket kits are available to upgrade the points to electronic ignition and these are commonly used by classic racers.

8.12 Here, you can see two sets of new contact breaker points with condensers. Note the small piece of felt: this should have 2-3 drops of light oil applied to it to lubricate the cam a little.

8.13 Always fit a new set of sparkplugs. Much attention is given to setting ignition timing and the points gap, but if the sparkplugs are in poor condition, your efforts to set them will be in vain.

8.14 The last part of the ignition system is the HT coil, which, if faulty, should be renewed. Hidden underneath the fuel tank, it does not normally give problems, even after years of use. The HT coil is solid state and not serviceable. This is an aftermarket coil, and widely available.

8.15 The HT caps should be changed if there are any cracks. These simply screw into the end of the HT lead.

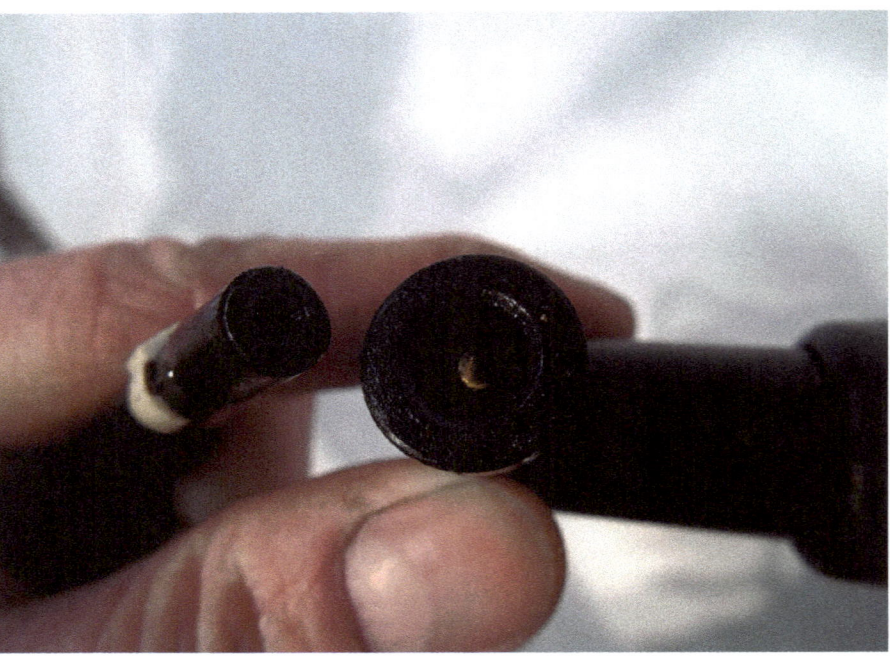

8.16 Check that the screw in the HT cap makes a good connection with the HT wire inside the HT lead. If there is no connection there will be no spark. You can snip off a small piece from the end of the HT lead if the screw inside the cap does not reach the wire inside the lead, but be careful not to cut off too much as this could make the lead too short to reach the sparkplug.

ELECTRICS

THE CHARGING AND STARTING SYSTEMS

Other than the brushes on the starter motor, these two systems are not serviceable, and usually give years of problem-free service. If faulty, however, replacement is the only option.

Those parts of the electrical system that are most commonly replaced are set out below.

8.17 Problems with an electric starter could indicate that the starter motor solenoid – between the starter motor and the battery – is at fault. When the starter button is pressed the solenoid should click; if it doesn't, test it as described in the workshop manual. One simple check is to ensure the battery is fully charged, and that the solenoid is earthed properly, as it could simply be a bad earth.

8.19 The voltage regulator takes a varying voltage and regulates it to a fixed voltage. Short circuits can cause problems with the regulator. If problems are suspected, refer to the workshop manual. This regulator is colour-coded to show where to connect the correct wires.

8.18 This is the rectifier unit. If you have a dead battery, or one that discharges quickly, it could be due to the rectifier. Again, refer to the workshop manual.

8.20 The alternator stator is housed behind this side casing, and gives few problems, which is just as well as it has no serviceable parts. Refer to the workshop manual for the testing procedure should you have concerns regarding the alternator.

HOW TO RESTORE HONDA FOURS

8.21 The starter motor has brushes, which are not difficult to replace.

8.22 Undo the two screws and remove the starter end housing to gain access to the brushes.

8.23 If the end is stuck, tap gently with a mallet.

8.24 Here, you can see the starter motor brushes held by coil springs. Replace the brushes if worn below the limit given in the workshop manual. In this case, this was 10mm.

8.25 The commutator copper will almost certainly be covered in black carbon dust. Clean with white spirit until bright and shiny.

ELECTRICS

8.28 Lastly, replace the top and tighten both crosshead screws. Make sure that the starter body is facing the right way so that the two screw holes are to the top when the starter is refitted to the engine, otherwise it won't be possible to refit the starter motor cover.

8.26 If the brushes need replacing, release their springs, unscrew the small crosshead screws and pull out the brushes. These brushes are long and in good condition.

8.27 When refitting the cover, remember to replace the washers in the reverse order to which they were removed.

Chapter 9
Spraying, decals & badges

Many parts on your project bike were originally painted or lacquered, and will almost certainly be in poor condition: scratched, chipped, or faded. Likewise, the decals will almost certainly require replacement at some point, especially if you decide that the tank needs repainting. In this chapter we go through the process of respraying these parts, replacing the decals, and restoring your bike to its original finish.

Parts that are usually painted or powder-coated –
- Fuel tank
- Side panels
- Frame
- Swinging arm
- Side and main stands
- Footrest brackets
- Top and bottom yokes
- Rear torque arm
- Battery compartment
- Air filter box
- Fork ears (headlamp brackets)
- Fork leg shrouds
- Headlamp cowl
- Brake callipers
- Speedo and tachometer housing
- Seat base
- Handlebar switch gear
- Engine mounting brackets

9.1 This Honda CB350 Four has great paintwork and decals, showing what can be achieved by respraying. The tank and side panels draw admiring glances, but parts such as the headlamp brackets, fork leg covers, and chain guards are often forgotten. Paying attention to these areas and making a good job of them will give your project a much better overall finish.

Preparation and painting is the same whatever component is resprayed. Note in particular where decals are placed – maybe take a photo you can refer to later for positioning. It may also be useful to take measurements of decal positions for later reference.

Remember that fumes from thinners and paints are dangerous

SPRAYING, DECALS & BADGES

and highly flammable. 2-pack paints should only be used by professionals with the appropriate safety equipment (worthwhile as these are more durable, and can be more highly polished than other paints). Aerosol and cellulose paints are more appropriate for DIY use, but do not use near naked flames or sparks, and wear an appropriate face mask at all times. Speak to your paint provider if you are not sure which mask to use. Likewise, when sanding, use an appropriate dust particle mask as sanding dust can damage your health.

TOOLS AND MATERIALS NEEDED

9.2 A wide range of paintshop products are required to complete the project. Because the majority of motorcycle parts are small, spray cans can produce good results if you don't have spray equipment.

Preparation
Sander, filler, cellulose putty, wet and dry paper (grades 120, 240, 500), dust particle mask, de-greaser.

Priming
Spray aerosol primer or compressor and spray gun, primer, thinners, tack cloth, spray mask. Strainer if you are using a spray gun.

Finish coat
The same tools that you used when priming, finish paint, 1200 grade wet and dry paper and polishing compound.

Let's start with the fuel tank, which is often the main focus of attention, and must look good. Once the tank is completely empty of fuel and cleaned inside, as described in the fuel and exhaust systems chapter, remove the fuel tap, cap, and all badges or decals to leave a completely bare tank.

If using spray cans, many paint suppliers will mix the colour you require, and send it to you in an aerosol. Because the area that needs spraying is relatively small on a motorcycle, buying spray equipment is not usually an option. If you already have spray equipment the preparation and spraying process is the same as described for cans.

STRIPPING PAINT
Preparation is paramount, and will reflect in the quality of the finished paint surface. With parts in a very bad condition – the fuel tank, for instance – it's worth spending the extra time to strip it back to bare metal (do not use paint stripper on any plastic parts).

9.3 Proprietary paint strippers for car body panels are suitable for stripping paint from any of the metal parts on the bike.

Chemical stripper is very strong, so follow the manufacturer's safety instructions. Gloves, goggles and good ventilation are essential.
The process for paint stripping is as follows.

9.4 Lightly brush the solution onto the part. After a little while the paint will start to bubble and blister. Once the entire part has been covered with stripper, begin to scrape off the paint with a paint scraper.

9.5 This will remove almost all of the paint; some difficult-to-reach areas may need another coat. You can get into awkward corners with a small wire brush or some wire wool.

Next, wash the part thoroughly with water (this neutralises the stripper), and dry it.

9.6 Once the part is dry, take a closer look at it. Dents will require filler to return the tank to its original shape.

Using a 2-part car body filler, follow the instructions and smooth the filler into each dent, leaving filler slightly proud of the tank surface. If the dent is large, build the filler in layers. When the filler has completely set, begin to sand the filled areas (wear a dust mask and goggles) with wet and dry abrasive paper. Start with a reasonably coarse grade of 120 to get the basic shape. Use a rubber sanding block if you find it easier, and keep the paper wrapped around it. Go over the area again with progressively finer grades of wet and dry: after grade 120 use 240, then 500, and finish with 1200. Keep the paper wet when sanding, as this helps prevent it from becoming clogged with filler residue.

If it's not possible to suspend the

HOW TO RESTORE HONDA FOURS

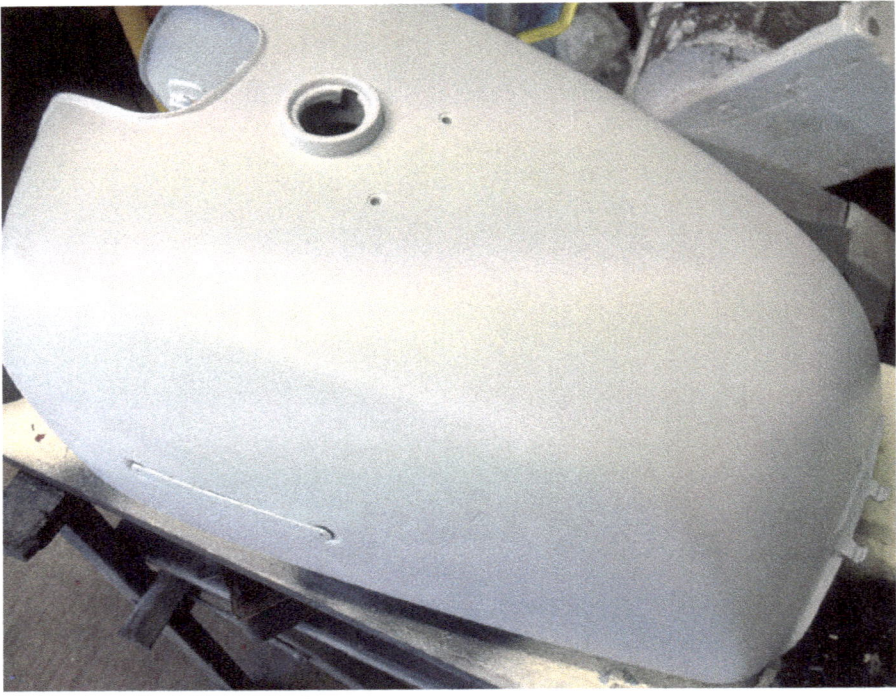

9.7 Dents filled, this tank has been completely sanded. The next stage is to dry it thoroughly, and spray on the first coat of primer. (Spraying should only be carried out in a well ventilated area, and wearing the appropriate safety mask and goggles.) Spray fumes should not be inhaled. Follow the instructions on the can.

9.9 Some parts can be suspended from a piece of strong cord or wire, which will allow you to spray all sides, on top, and underneath without moving or touching it.

tank, spray the underneath first and, once completely dry, turn it over and spray the top and sides. Allow both primer and finish paint to completely dry between coats. If the paint is still slightly wet and you apply more paint, runs will occur, which will mean starting again after these have been sanded out.

9.8 A CB350 Four tank rubbed down after the first coat of primer.

9.10 Application of a few coats of primer will show up small imperfections: fill and rub down.

9.11 Use fine surface body filler and go over these with a fine wet and dry paper, keeping the paper wet until the area is smooth again. Now apply two other coats of primer.

SPRAYING, DECALS & BADGES

Continue this process until there are no imperfections and the tank is completely smooth and fully primed. If you come across very small scratches or dents, use more fine filler or cellulose putty. This is applied lightly with a small plastic spatula and is pressed into the scratches or dents: it usually dries quite quickly.

9.12 Here, you can see a scratch that has been filled with fine cellulose putty.

Now that you have the tank 100 per cent smooth and fully primed, move on to the finish coats. Carefully wipe the tank, using a tack cloth to remove any fine dust from the area to be sprayed.

9.13 Apply 2-3 coats of finish paint, allowing each to dry completely before applying the next coat. Look carefully at each coat to check for dust or runs. If the finish has an orange peel texture, another rub over with a fine grade wet and dry paper is called for.

If this is your first spray attempt and you're happy with the results, well done: give yourself a pat on the back. It's not easy, first time round, and if you've achieved a good result now, chances are this will only get better. Don't worry too much if the end result is not 100 per cent. It's your first attempt, and runs, dust and the orange peel effect are common, and can all be dealt with. If there are runs, lightly rub down affected areas and respray.

The orange peel effect can be flatted with a very fine wet and dry paper when the paint has cured. The paint needs to be hard before you can begin cutting back. Leave as long as recommended by the manufacturer.

After a few attempts you will have a finished tank with no blemishes. If using metallic paint, follow the finish coat with two coats of lacquer to achieve the final shine. Lacquer can also be flatted and polished but, as with the top coat, leave until the lacquer has hardened fully.

Once the last coats are hardened – whether lacquer or paint – go over the whole tank with a fine rubbing compound or 2000 grit paper and a soft block until you have a high shine.

Make sure whenever you rub down or polish that the surface is completely free from any particles that could cause scratches to your finished work.

Once spraying is finished it's time to turn attention to badges and decals, to complete the appearance of your bike.

9.14 These CB350F side panels and fork leg shrouds were painted the same way as the tank.

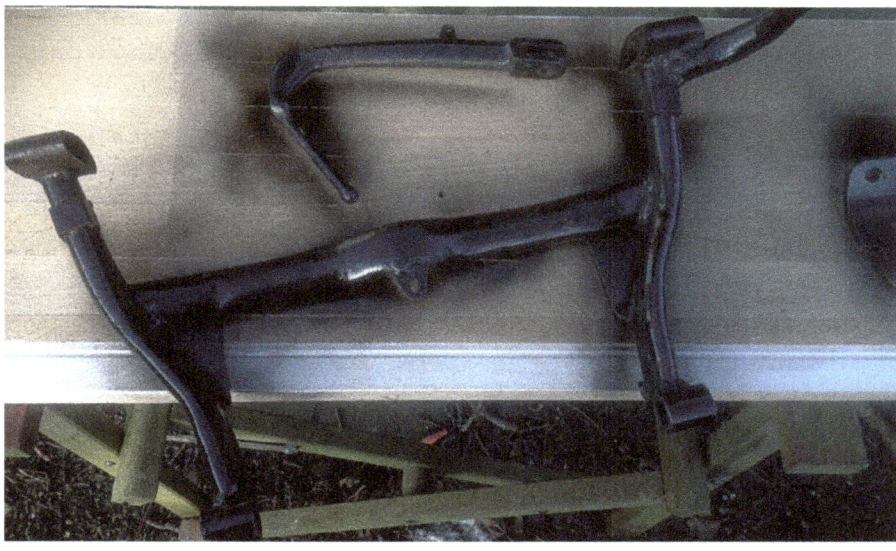

9.15 Don't forget to paint the smaller parts of your project, such as stands and brackets.

HOW TO RESTORE HONDA FOURS

FITTING THE DECALS

All motorcycles have decals. Some are purely decorative – such as pinstriping – whilst others provide information such as tyre pressures, and other safety warnings. To make your bike look as original as possible try to locate the decals for your model. Many companies reproduce exact copies of original decals, and most are small stickers that peel off a backing paper and simply stuck to the bike. With vinyl decals the technique is more involved, and can be quite challenging to get it right.

I will describe two methods of fitting the tank decal to your bike. One is demonstrated on a Suzuki tank that had just been sprayed; the other on a CB750 tank that was in reasonable condition, paint-wise.

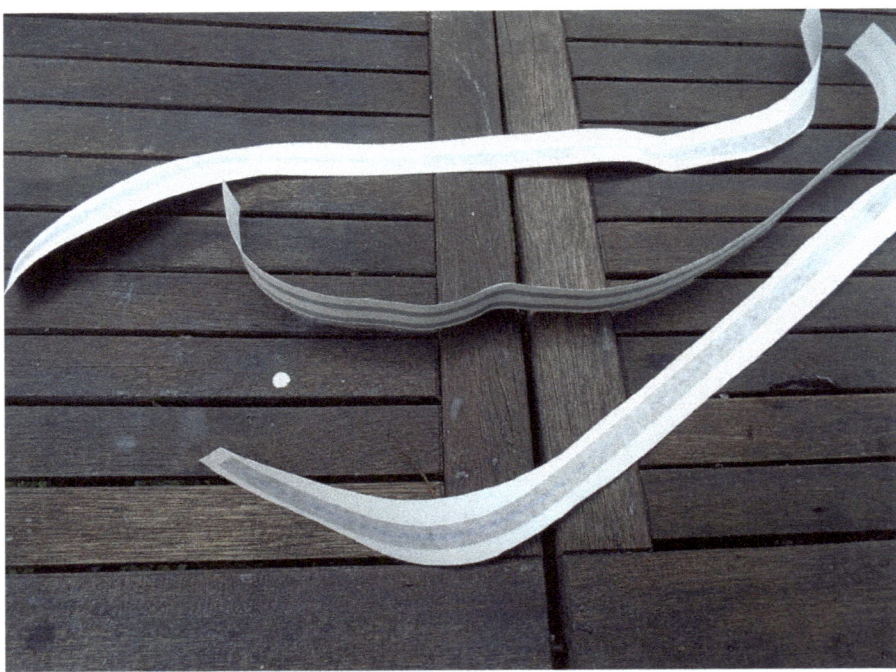

9.17 These stripes do not look much to start with, and come either folded or rolled. Be careful when opening the package as I have known people to cut open the package and cut through the new decal at the same time. Unfold the stripes and place on a flat surface as this helps them resume their original shape, and prevents the edges lifting during application.

The first method on the Honda CB750 tank uses a thick, vinyl stripe.

9.16 A variety of sticker decals for a Honda CB400F. These consist of all the original caution and advisory notices, as well as replacement speedometer and tachometer faces.

There are two main methods of applying decals: wet and dry. Both are essentially the same procedure but using the wet method does give a little more time for final positioning of the decal.

The main rules

Do a practice run first, and position the decal without sticking it, so you have an idea where it will go. Relax, take your time, if you rush you'll make mistakes.

Tools required –
- Craft knife
- Small garden sprayer
- Lint-free cloth

9.18 Establish fixed points to measure from.

SPRAYING, DECALS & BADGES

9.19 If there's more than one stripe, measure and note the distance between them.

9.20 Take plenty of measurements. The more you take the more accurately placed your new stripe will be.

9.21 Peel off the old decal ...

9.22 ... and use thinners to clean off the old glue.

All decals come on a paper backing, some of which fit the decal exactly and do not need to be cut back, but others have a much wider backing paper that should be trimmed before you attempt to fit the decal.

Assuming your decal has wide backing paper, cut it back as close to the decal as you can, making sure not to damage the decal.

Add a couple of drops of washing-up liquid to the garden sprayer and fill with cold water. Lightly spray the solution over the tank.

HOW TO RESTORE HONDA FOURS

9.23 Using the measurements taken earlier, and with the backing paper still on the decal, use masking tape to tape it in exactly the required position.

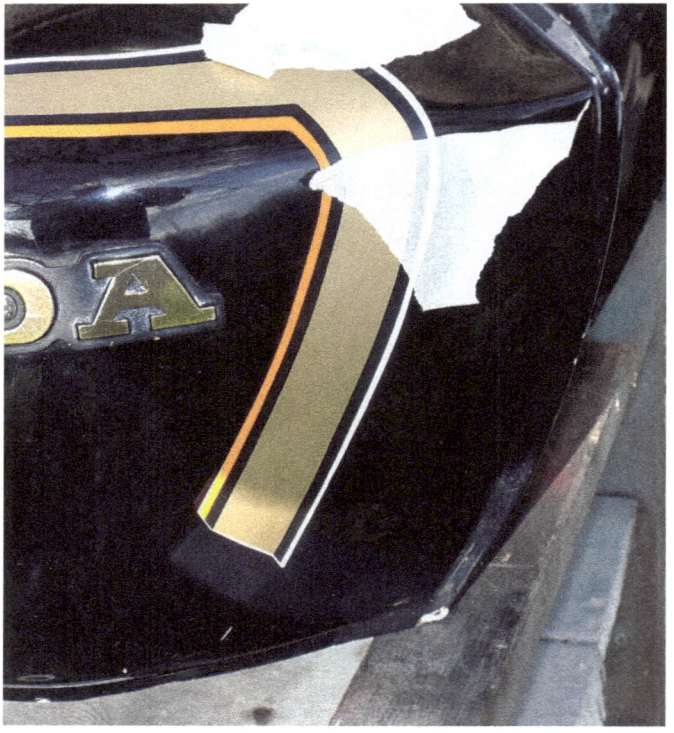

9.24 Most decals are shaped to lie flat in one way only, and, if fitted incorrectly, will crease. With this in mind, peel back 15mm of the backing paper and stick the decal to the tank, ensuring it lies flat and does not contain any air bubbles.

9.25/9.26 With the first part of the decal fixed to the tank, slowly peel back the rest of the backing paper and stick the decal to the tank a little bit at a time, ensuring that you do not distort the natural shape and fall of the decal (check this against your other measurements).

SPRAYING, DECALS & BADGES

9.27 Use a craft knife to trim any excess.

9.28 The finished decal. In most cases it's advisable to give the tank two coats of lacquer to protect the decal.

The second method is used with a vinyl decal that is much thinner, and is almost like applying several layers of paint. The decal is much more delicate than that used on the Honda tank, and is like a child's paper tattoo, where the paper peels off, leaving the decal adhered to the surface below.

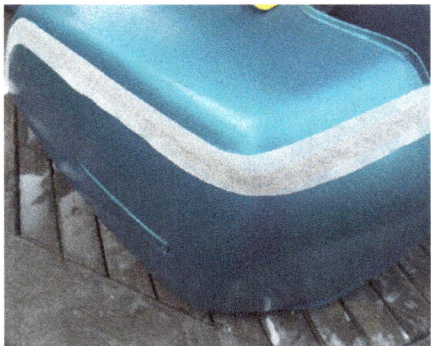

9.29 Lightly spray the tank with water and position the stripes lightly on the tank. Then, with a pencil, make small marks on the tank to highlight the points measured (this will help locate the decal in the right position).

9.30 Lastly, peel off the top layer of paper to reveal the finished stripe.

9.31 Wipe with a lint-free cloth to dry the area.

HOW TO RESTORE HONDA FOURS

9.32 If you have two stripes, overlap them at the corner, and trim to a clean edge with a craft knife.

9.33 That's it, you've just applied the decal yourself – more money saved. With a couple of coats of lacquer this tank will look like new.

Next, remove the backing paper from the decal and carefully stick it onto the tank using the pencil lines as a guide. Now press the decal firmly all over, being careful not to stretch or scratch it.

Badges

Badges and decals are a way for Honda to really get its marketing message across. Honda badges such as Super Sport, Custom and the engine size of the bike, followed by 'Four' are all designed to grab attention, and often advertise some of the main features of the motorcycle.

Honda changed the style and colour of badges and decals with every model version launched, and some will be difficult to find now.

9.34 This is one of my favourite badges from a Honda CB350 Four. Badges on later models are really only decals, but on earlier models they were much more elaborate, and decorative – raised embossed affairs that were very attractive.

A set of badges in original condition can fetch a good price on auction websites, because they are becoming more and more difficult to find. Some are reproduced and available, but often these are of poor quality. I know of some that do not even align with the locating holes on the side panels, meaning the buyer has to cut off the locating pins and glue the badge in position.

We can have some success restoring badges, particularly if they are metal or alloy.

SPRAYING, DECALS & BADGES

9.35 All resprayed with decals and badges in place, and looking very smart.

Chapter 10
Clocks & switches

The clocks (instruments) and switches on your restoration motorcycle will invariably require refurbishing. Some switches were anodised originally, whilst others were painted black. The paint will be worn, flaky, and looking pretty dull, at best, the clock surrounds are likely to be rusty around the edges, and the faces of the dials could be faded by the sun after years of exposure.

Let's start by generally assessing the switch gear. Are the switches complete with all switch covers and buttons, and do they still operate? Are all the wires there, and do they have their connectors?

Remove all switch gear from the bike and find a clean space for it on your workbench. Some switch gear parts are very small so good lighting will be helpful when working with these. Springs are a particular problem, so be careful when pulling apart the switch gear. Take photos as you proceed so that you know where all the small pieces go when it comes to reassembly. Most workshop manuals don't show a detailed strip down of the switch gear so photos will be very helpful in this respect.

10.0 Honda switch gear that has seen better days.

10.2 Disconnect the wiring connector that is hidden inside the headlamp shell.

10.1 Unscrew the two screws holding together the halves of the switch body. Look out for any broken pieces or springs which may drop out.

10.3 With the switch on the bench, open the switch body: it will probably be full of dirt and cobwebs.

CLOCKS & SWITCHES

10.4 Carefully dismantle and remove all the internal parts from the main body.

10.5 The engine stop switch has to be de-soldered to remove completely, but masking tape can be used to cover those areas not being painted.

10.6 Once apart your switch unit will look like this. Be sure to use the correct size screwdriver on these tiny screws, as they are not very forgiving if you use the wrong size, and will round off very quickly. The correct size screwdriver and a firm hold will crack the join between the head of the screw and the body, avoiding having to drill out screws that have snapped or rounded off. Unscrew all the screws and store: a small plastic container for each switch is a good idea. Try not to mix up the screws and springs between different sets of switch gear.

10.7 Some parts are extremely small – be careful not to lose them.

Give everything a thorough clean. De-grease the copper contact parts, and use some fine wet and dry paper to take the patina off the contact areas. Just sand lightly until the metal has a bright look to it again.

Blow out the dust from inside the empty switch unit body.

10.8 Using a small paintbrush clean everything in de-greaser, including the small parts, then wash in warm, soapy water and dry thoroughly.

This is the best opportunity for repainting the switchgear body, as there will be no masking up to do.

HOW TO RESTORE HONDA FOURS

10.9 There are several ways to remove old paint, but I have found the best method is to use paint stripper or a blast cabinet with a fine media.

Originally, some switches were anodised, whilst others were painted. One small aerosol can is sufficient for three coats on a good number of switches. Follow the instructions on the can: three coats are usually enough.

10.10 A gloss finish. These switch bodies were painted outside for good ventilation.

Once the paint has dried, move on to painting the letters. This is a fiddly task, and may take several attempts to get right, but will be worth the effort when you see the finished job.

You will need a small paintbrush and the correct colour paint. I find it easier to paint the lettering and wipe off any excess, as it's almost impossible to paint the letters without getting [paint on the newly-painted body.

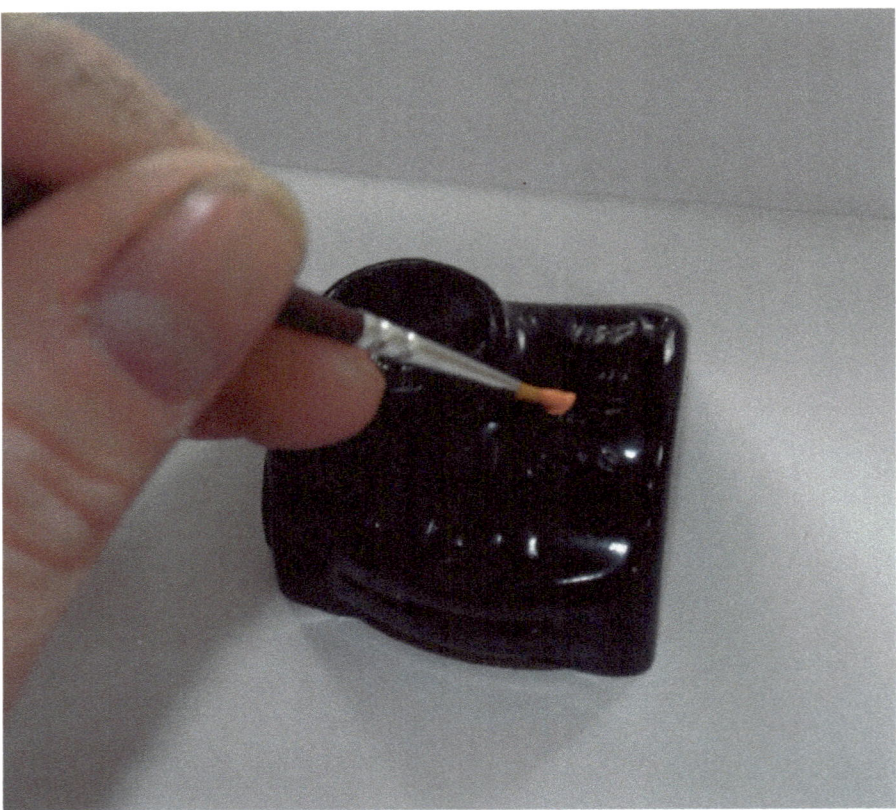

10.11 Paint with a small brush, then wipe off the excess.

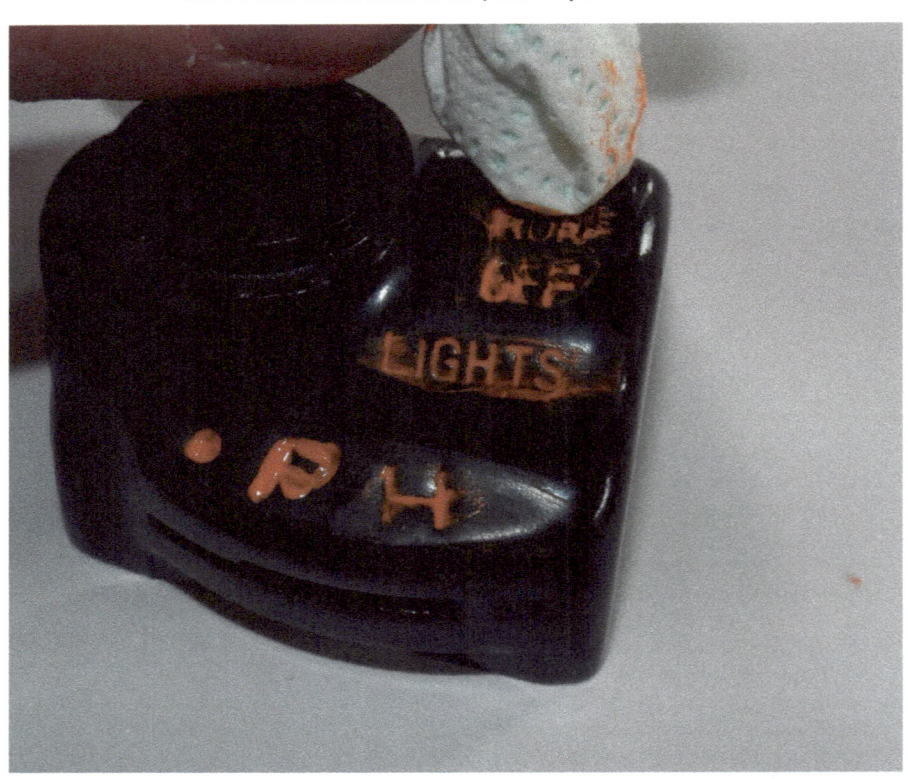

10.12 Wiping off the excess paint.

CLOCKS & SWITCHES

You may need to apply more than one coat of paint, but let it dry and check the results. When happy, rebuild the switch gear, ready to go on the bike later.

10.13 The letters after just one coat of paint. Looking good already.

REBUILDING THE SWITCH GEAR

When reassembling everything, apply a tiny amount of grease to those moving parts that will wear. Be careful not to get grease on the copper or brass contact parts.

There is a correct order for reassembly, and if you have taken photos while dismantling the switch gear, it will be easier to rebuild.

During reassembly look out for small slots in the alloy body where the switch parts fit: the switch will not work correctly if the parts are not properly fitted in the slot.

10.15. Insert the headlight switch. Note the two positioning slots and that the plastic knob should be facing in the 'up' position.

10.14 Begin by fitting the engine stop switch. This simply pushes in, and is held by a small spring clip at the back.

10.16 Replace the headlight switch arm with a small dome screw and washer, making sure it fits over the plastic knob.

HOW TO RESTORE HONDA FOURS

10.17 Replace the cable holder.

10.18 With the cable holder fitted, the headlamp arm should move freely over the top, as shown here.

10.19 Replace the horn button with its spring. Here, you can see the two slots where the switch is inserted.

10.20 This is how the two parts of the horn button must be positioned before fitting in the housing. The metal part fits behind the slot nearest to the horn button, while the other part fits into the slot nearest the inside of the body.

10.21 Once the switch is back in place, screw it in and refit the cable holder. This part of the switch is now rebuilt.

10.22 The switch gear rebuilt and repainted, looking like new.

CLOCKS & SWITCHES

CLOCKS AND GAUGES

Just like the switch gear, clocks and gauges can be restored to reasonable condition quite easily and cheaply during a general cosmetic overhaul. Note, though, that if either (or both!) the speedometer or tachometer do not work, it's much easier to find replacements than to repair them.

Generally speaking, clocks and gauges will still work okay, even after long periods of inactivity, and only the dial faces, paintwork, and maybe the glass that needs attention.

If the dial face has faded you can either live with it or attempt to improve it, and how successful the latter course of action is will depend on how badly it has faded, and how good you would like the overall finish to be.

Dial faces are available online for most motorcycles, and fitting these means stripping the clocks. Many clocks were not designed to be taken apart, and the biggest problem in this respect is that many have a pressed steel band around the base, holding it together.

10.24 Use a craft knife to cut the masking tape as close as possible to the edge.

If it's necessary to dismantle the clock, the procedure is as follows.

10.23 If the dial face is in a condition that's acceptable, it won't be necessary to dismantle the clock. Masking the glass and chrome ring, and simply re-spraying the clock is really the best approach, as dismantling and rebuilding it is not always successful.

10.25 Gently prise up the edge of the chrome ring all the way around until it can be lifted from the clock. Be very patient when doing this, taking care not to damage the chrome ring, as then it will be impossible to rebuild the clock.

HOW TO RESTORE HONDA FOURS

10.26 Before the housing can be removed, unscrew this tiny screw and remove the milometer knob.

10.29 Unscrew the bolts at the back and remover the chrome cover.

10.27 The speedo and tacho needles simply prise off.

10.30 Once the housing is off, remove the glass and prepare the housing for painting.

10.28 The faceplate screws are removed next.

10.31 The clock housing is in three parts.

CLOCKS & SWITCHES

10.32 The inner housing will not require painting, and really only supports the glass.

10.33 Clean the glass before putting it back on the inner housing; note the rubber seal.

10.34 The outer housing is then placed over the top of the glass.

10.35 Stick on the new dial face and replace the screws and needle.

TIP! Position the new dial face over the old before removing the backing, and, with a small pin, make holes where the two screws go. This will help align the new dial face in exactly the right position.

10.36 The most difficult task is refitting the chrome band. This should be re-positioned and gently squeezed all around with a set of pliers until it is tight and holding the clock together. This is a delicate job, and care should be taken not to damage the ring. If you don't get this part right, it's unlikely the clock will ever go back together. In the case of the speedo remember to reinstate the milometer knob.

HOW TO RESTORE HONDA FOURS

10.37 If you cannot refit the chrome surround aftermarket clock covers are available. These have a screw on chrome ring that holds them in place.

10.39 Polish the chrome backing and refit to the clock.

10.38 These look very smart and are available in a black or chrome finish.

10.40 The tachometer with the new dial face in place, ready to go on the bike.

CLOCKS & SWITCHES

10.41 Clocks finished and refitted to the bike.

Chapter 11
The seat

Almost all restoration projects encounter problems with the rider's seat. The change between cold and warm weather conditions over a long period of time, or having been propped against a garage wall or shed, causes the cover to split or tear.

It is essential that the seat looks and feels right on your completed restoration: seats can be recovered, and if the splits/tears are not too big, the foam underneath may be in usable condition.

Foam is an easy material to work with, and if only a small repair is required it's quite simple to cut a suitably-sized piece and glue it into the damaged area. The seat cover, when fitted, will be tight and help hold the repair in place. However, if the foam has been exposed for too long it will not be repairable, and new seat foam will be required.

Seat covers are available for almost all motorcycles and are not difficult to fit, but ensure that you order the exact seat cover for your motorcycle model, year and type. I once ordered a seat cover for a Honda 1973 CB350T – a slightly different model to my 1973 CB350F – and had to buy a second cover after the first one tore while I was trying to 'make it fit.' Lesson learned!

11.1 It is not often that the foam is completely unusable, but if it has been exposed to sunlight, the UV rays will render it unusable.

11.2 Potentially the most problematic is the seat base. Most seats have pressed metal bases that rust over the years, and a badly-corroded base can often be irreparable. The hinges and brackets should be sound and firmly fixed to the base, because if they do not have a good fixing, repairing the base becomes necessary.

THE SEAT

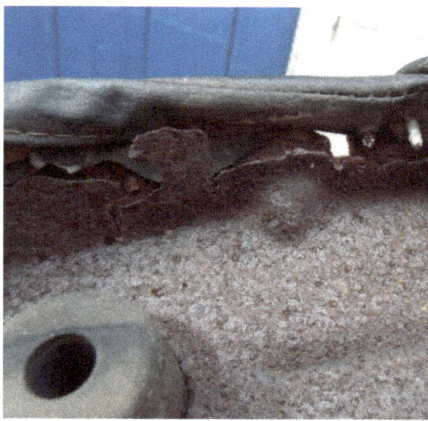

11.3 A seat base like this is too badly corroded to be repaired: the edge of the seat base has completely rusted away. Small holes can be covered by a plate, which will also restore some strength to that area, but more serious damage means another seat will be required.

11.4 This CB750 seat base is in good condition, showing only light rust. It is complete with hinges and catches, which are solidly attached to the seat base.

11.5 Also in very good condition are the seat rubbers that support the seat on the motorcycle frame.

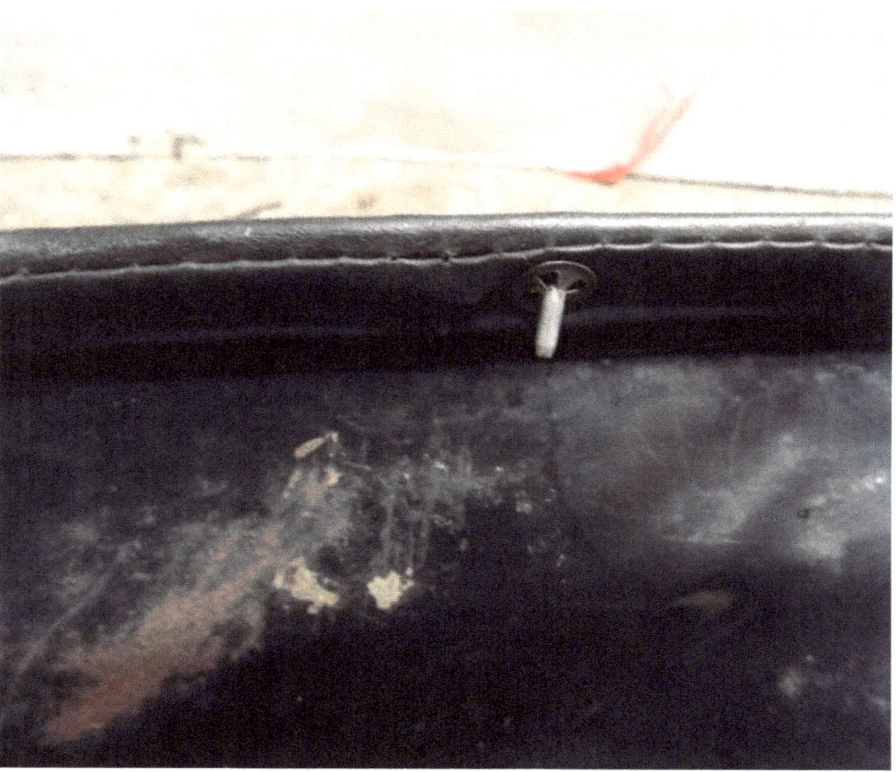

11.6 Here, we can see the alloy tab that holds the chrome seat trim in place. This often snaps off when trying to straighten it, so go easy. If you can straighten it try not to lose the spring washer.

11.7 The seat strap buckle is in good condition and should clean up quite nicely.

HOW TO RESTORE HONDA FOURS

11.8 Even the seat edging on this seat is in very good condition and fully attached with no damage.

11.10 Recovering this seat will restore it to usable condition: luckily, there's only minimal foam damage.

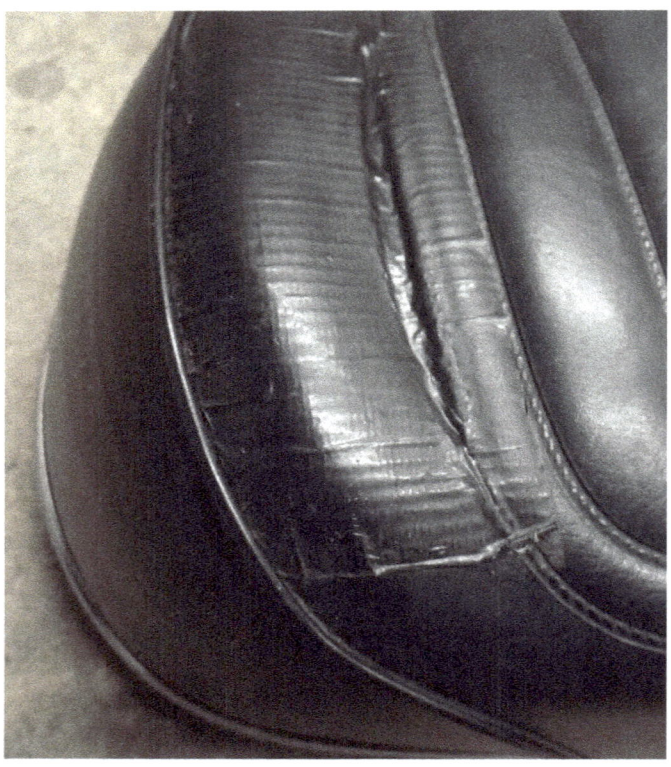

11.9 It's a shame that there's a split at the rear of this seat because, other than this, it's in very good condition. A seat like this is in usable condition, and can wait until the end of the project for attention.

11.12 The chrome-look trim on this seat is part of the cover: it's badly worn and the lettering is very faded.

THE SEAT

11.13 The seat has metal clasps which hook the cover all around the inside edge of the base, tightly holding it in place. Often, these clasps have broken or rusted away, but this clasp is in good condition.

11.15 With brackets and hinges removed, gently pull back all clasps with a pair of pliers. Do not bend back too far; just enough to clear the seat edge trim.

11.14 Start by unbolting all brackets and hinges ready for de-greasing and painting.

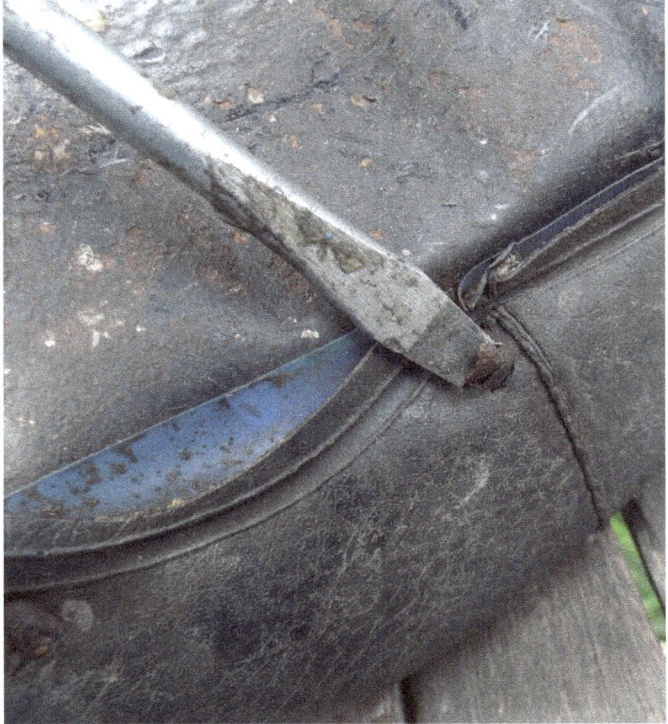

11.16 The smaller clasps are not as easy to get at with pliers, but a flat blade screwdriver or similar can be used to prise them up.

HOW TO RESTORE HONDA FOURS

11.17 If fitted, remove the strap to allow the seat cover to come off.

11.19 Pull the trim off the seat, working all the way around the seat base until the cover can be removed completely.

11.18 Some of these screws can be very tight, and a more forceful way of removing them could become necessary. This screw would not budge easily, and this was the only way to remove it, necessitating a new screw in the process.

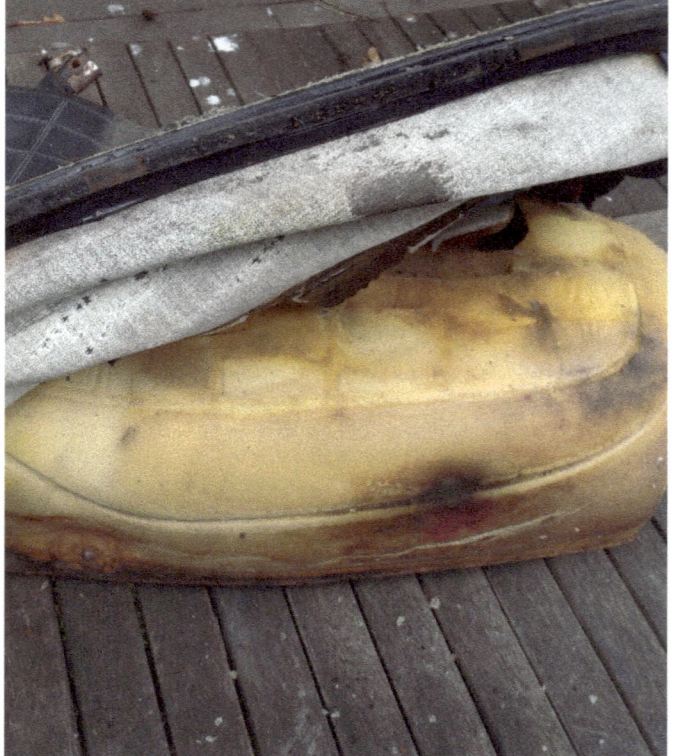

11.20 Pull off the seat cover, being careful not to damage the foam.

THE SEAT

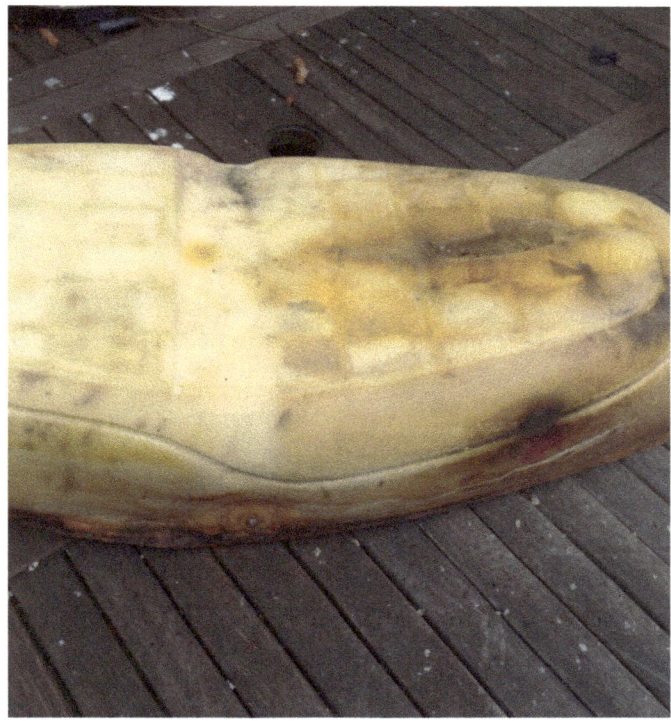

11.21 This seat foam is in relatively good condition considering it's 40 years old! It still has a good shape, and only minor damage has resulted from the tear.

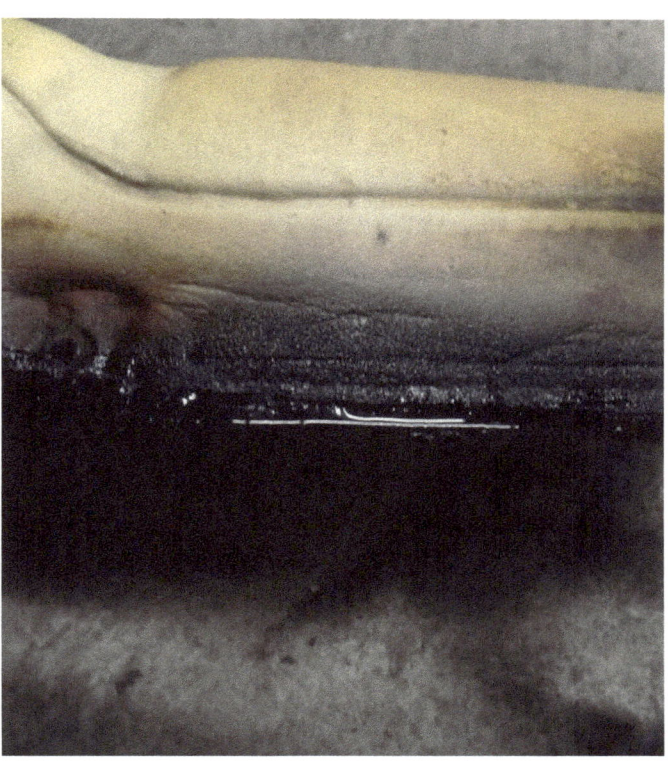

11.23 Paint or spray the edge once the rust is removed, providing a clean surface for the trim to stick to.

11.22 Clean the base edge to remove any rust before painting. Trim is glued on, so a sound surface to adhere to will be required.

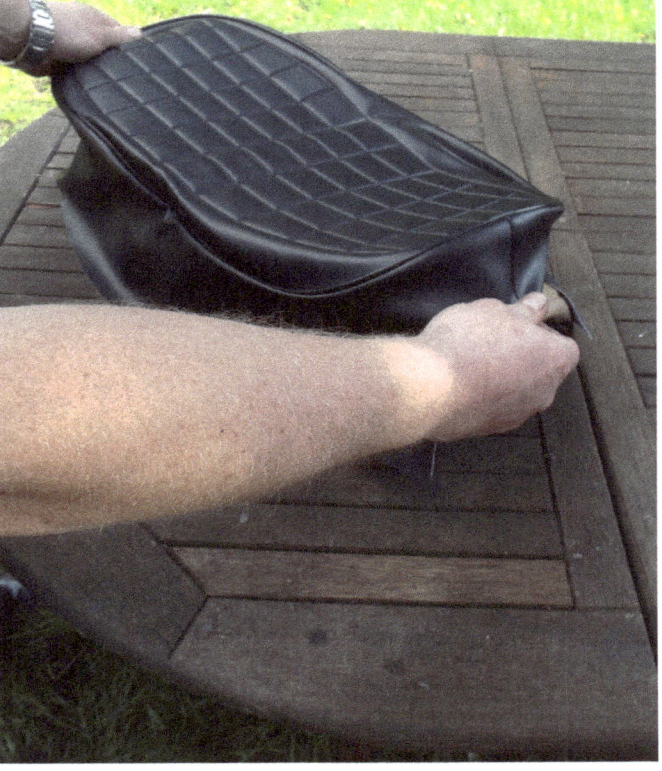

11.24 Loosely place the cover over the foam base.

HOW TO RESTORE HONDA FOURS

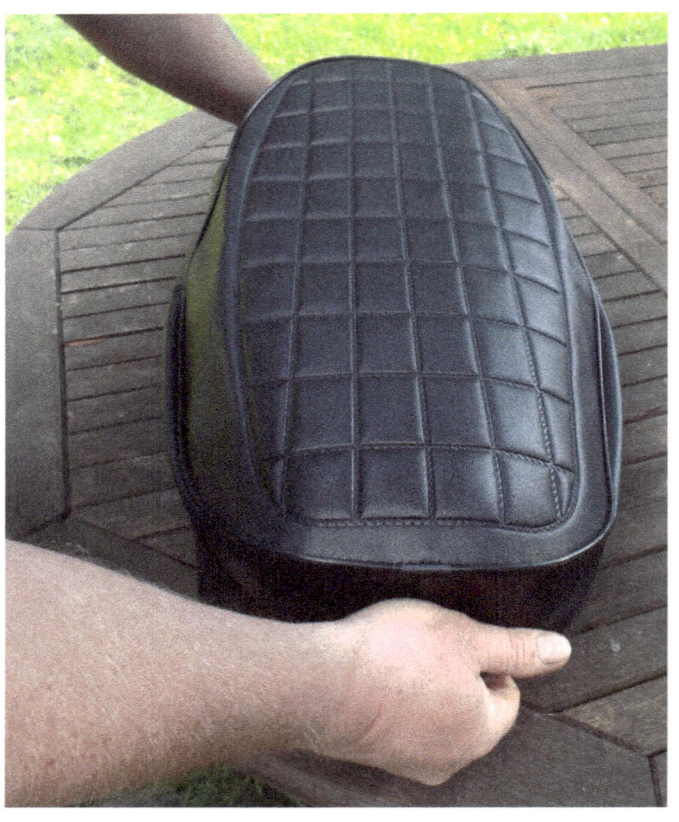

11.25 Pull the front and back of the cover so that the edging lines up with the profile of the seat. Do this on both sides so that the seat pattern is central to the top of the seat.

11.27 Work across the front of the seat until all the pointed clasps are through, and bend them so that they hold the seat cover in position.

11.26 With the cover pulled tightly at the front, pierce with the pointed clasps.

11.28 Do the same at the back and all around the edge with the bigger clasps.

THE SEAT

Original seat edge trim is almost impossible to find. However, there is an effective alternative. Car door edging is inexpensive, and very effective at providing your seat with an almost original trim look.

Some parts needed for your restoration may no longer be available, particularly smaller detail parts. In this case, an alternative replacement must be sourced which will replicate the original finish and quality.

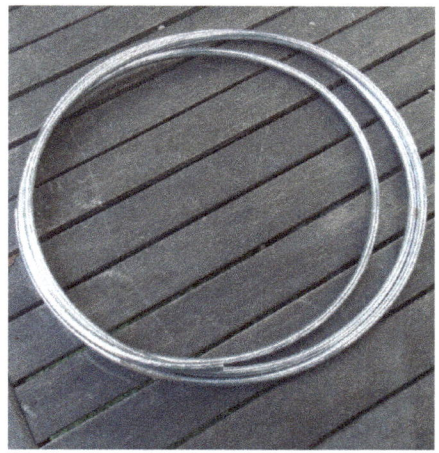

11.29 If you cannot source correct seat edging, car door trim can be an acceptable alternative.

11.31 Begin on one of the front corners, and push the trim over the edge of the seat; continue round to the other corner. Push down firmly: the trim has a snug fit and will hold the seat cover tightly in place.

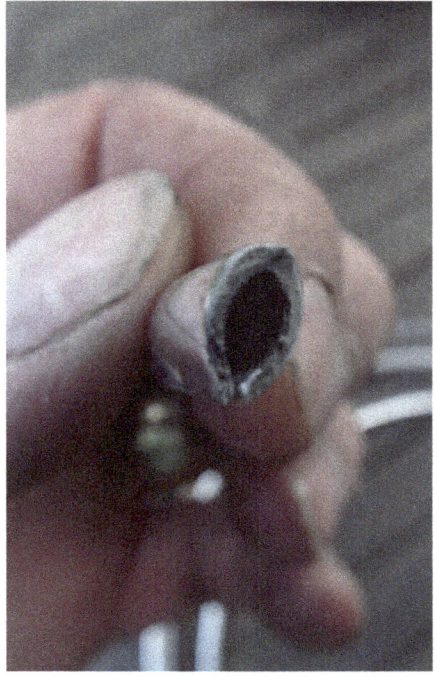

11.30 Car door edge trim is open at the bottom, and filled with glue inside.

11.32 With a sharp pair of scissors, cut the front edge to the same angle as the front of the seat.

135

HOW TO RESTORE HONDA FOURS

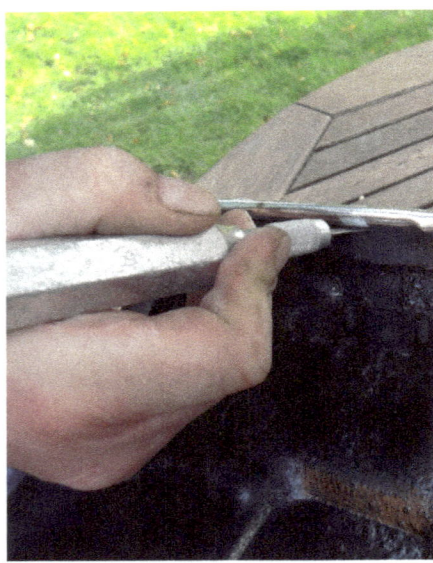

11.33 Now trim off any excess material under the chrome trim edge with a craft knife, to leave a nice, clean finish.

11.34 Almost finished, the seat is looking like new. Add the strap and it's done.

11.35 Because the original seat strap screws are no longer available, a suitable replacement had to be found.

11.36 Three stainless steel coach bolts were found, and the thread was cut to the full length of the bolt.

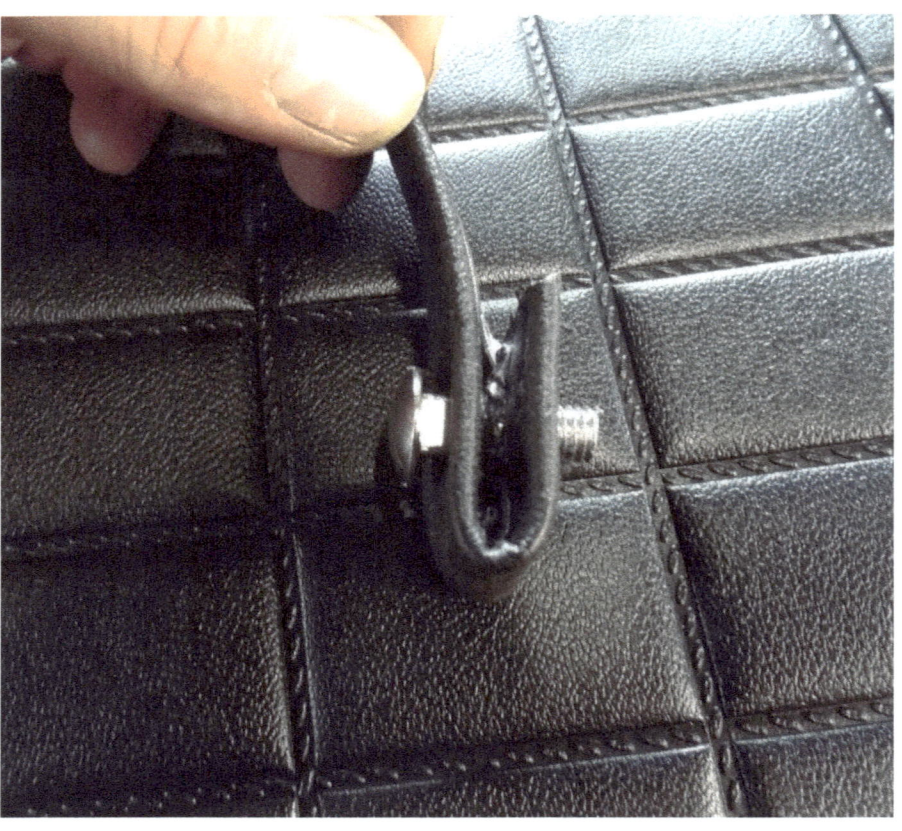

11.37 The bolt was then cut to the length required, and pushed through the folded strap.

THE SEAT

11.38 The thread on the original nut (which is welded to the seat base) was damaged, so it was drilled out and a new stainless steel nut used.

11.40 Lettering standing out proud again.

11.41 A Honda seat showing the new chrome trim, lettering, and strap.

11.39 The finished seat with the strap now fitted, and looking very respectable.

Chapter 12
The forks

All Honda SOHC Fours used telescopic forks with hydraulic damping, and this chapter covers the strip and rebuild of a pair of these.

Note: before attempting to rebuild the front forks, check for scratches on the stanchions, as these will cause damage to the fork oil seal, necessitating a regrind of the stanchions and plating by a specialist. It is pointless fitting new seals if this reconditioning hasn't been carried out beforehand as the seal will simply fail again. It will be necessary to strip the forks in order to send the stanchions for refurbishment.

It is common to find that fork oil has leaked out or broken down, making it unusable. Replace with the correct grade of oil and top up to the correct level, as advised by the workshop manual.

The following picture sequence identofies fork components and shows the procedure for dismantling and rebuilding a front fork.

12.1 The fork leg: this is the part that will be polished and which the stanchions slide into. The fork seals sit inside the top of the fork leg.

THE FORKS

12.2 Remove the small bolt to drain the fork oil.

12.3 The stanchion: this is the part that is chrome plated and which slides into the fork leg. If this part is scratched it will damage the seal and lead to an oil leak. The stanchion often has a cover to protect it, in the form of either a rubber gaiter or a painted metal shroud. On later models, however, the stanchion was naked and more exposed to the elements.

12.4 A close-up of a stanchion shows rust and pit marks. This stanchion will need to be re-ground and chrome plated before we can rebuild this fork leg.

12.5 Drain the fork oil via the small bolt at the bottom of the fork leg, or invert to allow the oil to run out. Place a container (not glass) under the fork leg and drain the oil into this. You may have to compress the fork a little to expel all of the oil. This is why a glass container is not used, as it may break under the force.

12.6 Unscrew the top filler plug. Be aware that the plug will be under a little tension from the fork spring.

12.7 Once the filler plug is out, remove the fork spring. Even after draining the oil, more is likely to run out now, so have some cloth ready as it's a messy job.

HOW TO RESTORE HONDA FOURS

12.8 The coil spring will become compressed over time: check against the manufacturer's measurements in the workshop manual that it is still the correct length.

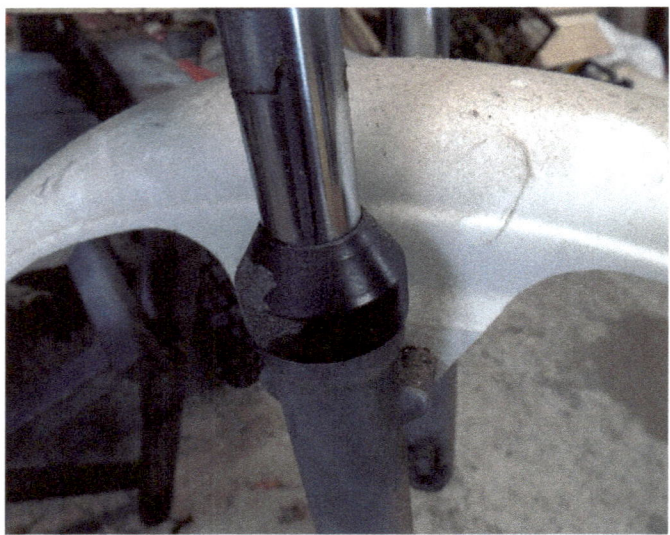

12.9 A fork leg that is leaking oil: replace the seal.

12.10 Next, remove the dust cover by prising it out of its slot and sliding it off the top of the fork leg.

12.11 Now we can see the circlip in the top of the fork leg. Clean off any visible rust.

12.12 Most models have a circlip. Holding the leg firmly, remove the circlip and give it a good clean.

THE FORKS

12.13 Others models have a wire clip which is much easier to remove.

12.14 There is an Allen bolt on the underside of the fork leg: remove this.

12.15 This Allen bolt is often very tight and may have never been removed before. It is important here to use the correct size Allen key. If this screw/bolt becomes rounded it will be very difficult to repair because of its location. You may need to hold the fork leg in a vice. Use plenty of cloth to avoid damaging the fork leg.

12.16 Withdraw the stanchion – sometimes a slide hammer action is needed here. If it's stuck you may need to clamp the leg in the vice before pulling out the stanchion.

12.17 Now that you can clearly see the seal, prise it out but be careful not to damage the seat.

141

HOW TO RESTORE HONDA FOURS

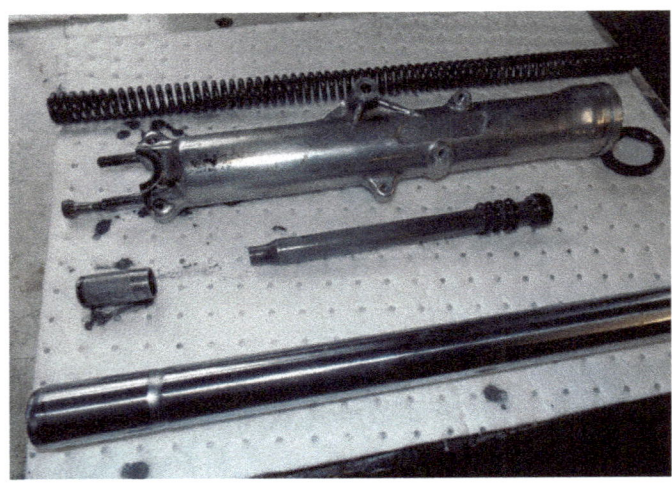

12.18 Clean all parts thoroughly ready for reassembly. This picture also shows the oil lock and the bottom pipe.

12.21 A pair of new fork seals will be required.

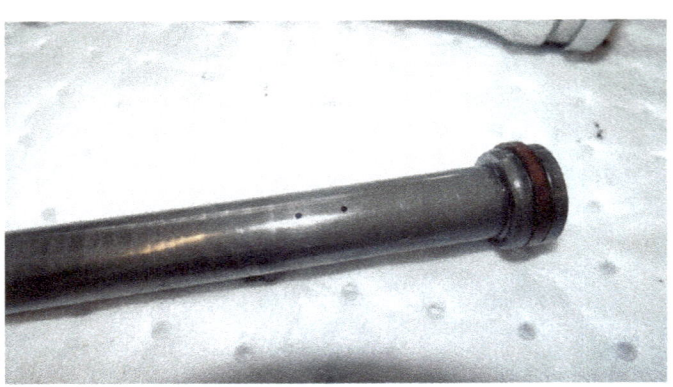

12.19 All holes must be clear of debris.

12.22 Place the new seal into the top of the leg; tap down evenly with a rubber mallet.

12.20 It is essential to ensurethat the seal recess is properly cleaned.

12.23 Replace the bottom pipe and spring in the stanchion.

THE FORKS

12.24 Now, with the bottom pipe all the way through the stanchion, replace the oil lock ...

12.26 Replace the filler plug (you may need to clamp the stanchion in a vice while you compress the spring).

12.25 ... then push the stanchion into the fork leg.

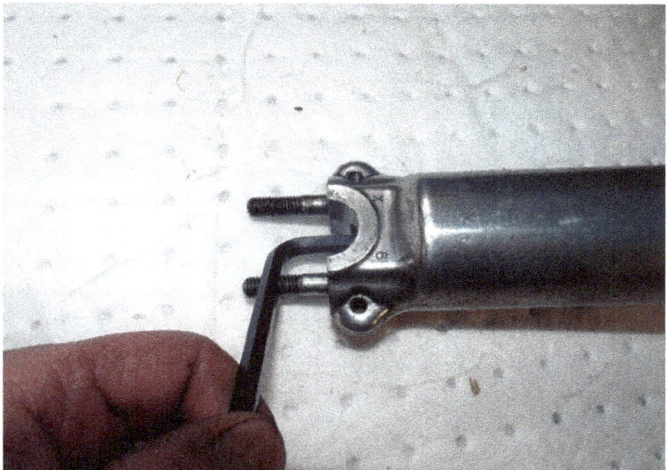

12.27 Next, tighten the Allen bolt. It helps to replace the filler plug first because this puts the oil lock under pressure and prevents it turning while you fit the bolt. Lastly, top up the forks with oil, using the measurement guide on the bottle. If it doesn't have a guide, a measuring jug is a good alternative.

www.velocebooks.com
New book news • Special offers • Newsletter • Details of all Veloce books • Gift Vouchers

Chapter 13
Rebuild

Once the frame has been powder-coated or resprayed, the rebuild can begin. Before you start, however, ensure that all nuts, bolts and washers are as clean as possible, or you have replacements ready to fit.

Some projects are rebuilt over a long period of time due to the difficulty in sourcing the parts required, but even if this is the case, you can still start the rebuild, and continue with it as and when parts become available. Fortunately, most Honda SOHC parts are available, albeit secondhand or refurbished items, which should allow fairly speedy completion of the project.

FRAME BUILD AND REAR END
Begin by raising the frame off the ground onto a solid platform with good support for when fitting the stands, swinging arm, and forks, etc.

13.0 Offer up the swinging arm and push it into place: you may need to use a rubber mallet to do this if the fit is a little tight.

REBUILD

13.1 Before fitting the swinging arm ensure that the dust covers are over the bushes.

13.2 Fit the swinging arm by lightly tapping the bolt through with a rubber mallet. Grease the bushes and the large swinging arm pivot bolt before fitting.

13.3 Tighten to the torque setting noted in the workshop manual. The swinging arm should move freely, with no perceptible side-to-side play.

A socket or spanner on both ends of the swinging arm bolt will prevent it turning while tightening.

13.4 Fit the stands while the frame is supported. Grease the eyes where the stand springs go through a little, and use a pair of good pliers to pull the return spring over the hook.

13.5 Next, fit both rear shock absorbers. The dome nuts on the top two mountings are original, but are often lost. Stainless steel dome nuts are available as an alternative, and will enhance the finished look.

145

HOW TO RESTORE HONDA FOURS

13.6 Check that the rubber bushes are in good condition, as poor examples will adversely affect handling.

13.9 The inner mudguard simply slots into the two small brackets on the inside of the frame.

13.7 The grab rail is next, and this attaches to the top shock absorber mounts and the two rear mudguard mounting bolts.

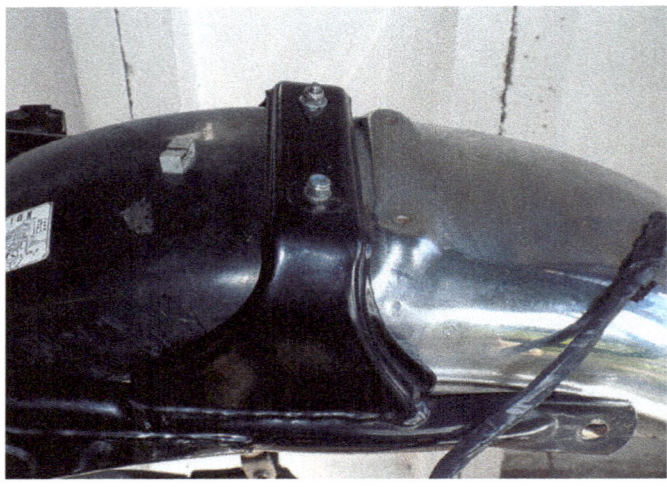

13.10 Once the plastic part of the mudguard is fitted, bolt on the chrome half, held by four bolts, two of which are on the rear of the frame, as shown here, and also retain the plastic mudguard.

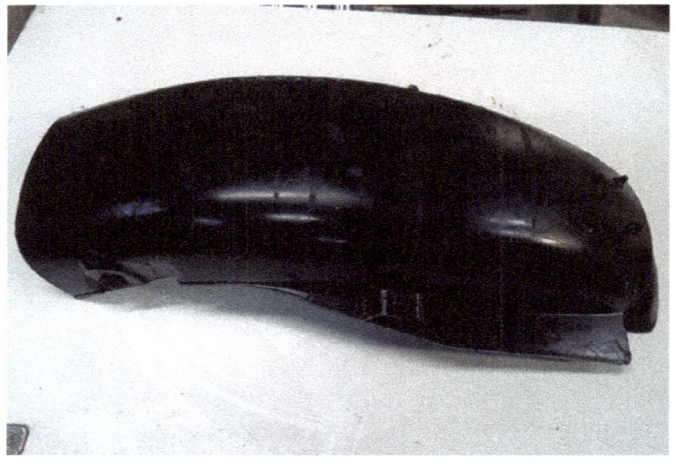

13.8 Replace the rear plastic inner mudguard.

13.11 The last two bolts go through the grab rail and screw into the mudguard.

REBUILD

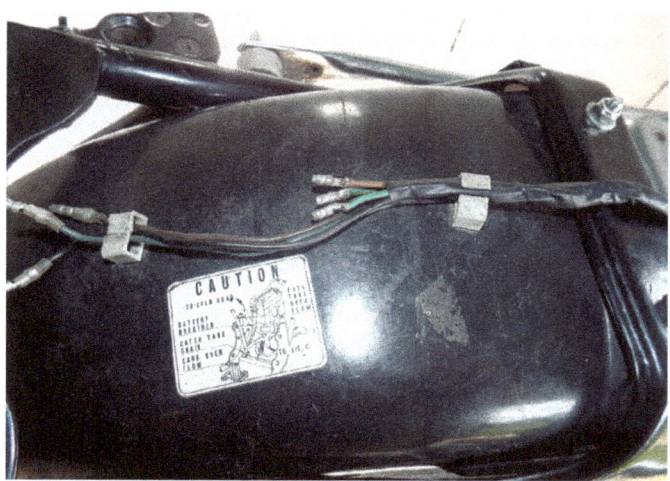

13.12 Make sure that the wires passing over the mudguard are free. Clip them in the cable guides as shown.

13.14a The seat lock can now be fitted. This is held on by two small screws.

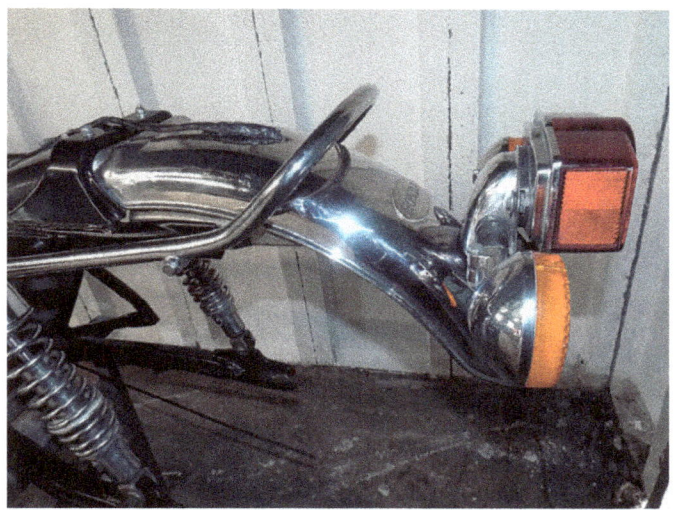

13.13 Attach the rear light unit and bracket ...

13.15 Bolt in place the coil pack before fitting the wiring loom.

13.14 ... via the three bolts that screw into the mudguard underneath at the rear.

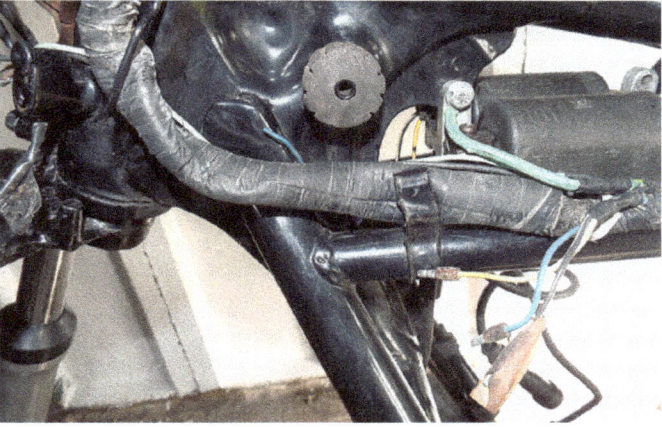

13.16 Fit the wiring loom along the entire length of the frame. If you do not have the original ties, use cable ties and snip off the ends to make them look neater.

HOW TO RESTORE HONDA FOURS

13.17 Refit the electrical panel and pass the two battery leads through into the battery compartment.

13.18 The electrical component panel and battery compartment is an all-in-one unit, held to the frame with rubber-mounted bolts.

13.19 Next, fit the fuel tank rubber.

13.20 The CB750 has an oil tank on this side, and on other models, this is where the battery compartment will go. If restoring a CB750, ensure the oil tank is flushed out and clean inside before fitting it back on the frame, as any debris inside will find its way into the engine.

REBUILDING THE FRONT END

All Honda SOHC Fours had ball bearings held in bearing carriers as standard in the steering stem. Taper roller bearings are available as an upgrade, and are usually fitted as part of a restoration.

13.21 If intending to fit taper bearings, note that these often sit slightly higher than the top of the frame when fitted, as shown in the picture. This is not a great problem although, when fitting the headlamp brackets, large O-rings for each fork leg will be necessary. These act as packing, taking up the slack caused by the taper bearing being a little high, and prevent the headlamp bracket from being loose.

REBUILD

13.22 Whichever type of steering bearings you have, clean thoroughly and check condition. Refer to your workshop manual and count how many ball bearings there are. Each model has a different number, and even top and bottom can be different to each other.

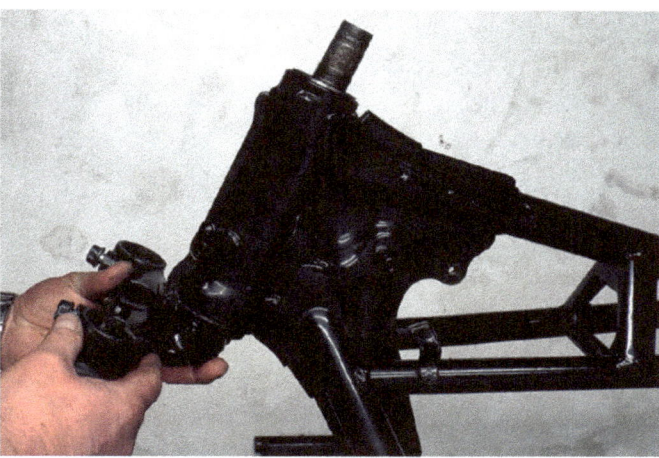

13.25 When inserting the steering stem, ensure that bearings don't fall out of the carriers. Carefully slide in the stem, trying not to allow the top to dislodge the bearings in the top yoke carrier.

13.23 When fitting the ball bearings apply plenty of grease to the bearing carriers, and ensure the bearings are cleaned and greased beforehand. The grease not only lubricates the bearings but also prevents them falling out whilst inserting the steering stem.

13.26 Now fit the dust cover and nut. Screw hand-tight for now.

13.24 Apply plenty of grease to the carrier on the bottom yoke, too, and place the bearings on the carrier.

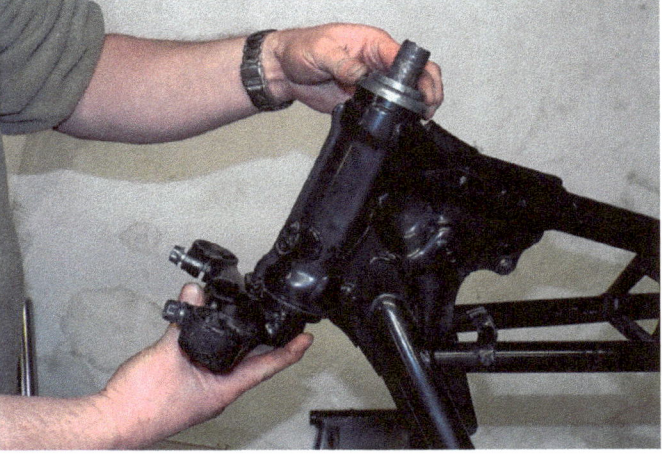

13.27 Support the stem from below until dust cover and nut are fitted. Using a C-spanner, tighten just enough so that no up and down movement in the steering stem is possible, but the stem still has free movement to turn without binding.

HOW TO RESTORE HONDA FOURS

If fitting taper roller bearings, remove the old ball bearing carriers using a strong piece of steel rod or similar to tap them out. Fitting the taper bearings is quite easy, but will require a piece of wood placed over the bearing that you gently tap in. Make sure to keep it square, because if it begins to go in at an angle it will jam: it is a very tight fit.

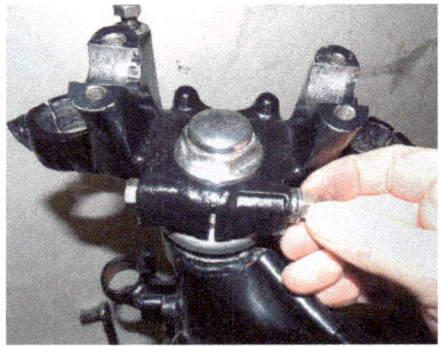

13.28 Next, fit the steering stem, the pinch bolt, nut and washer, and tighten.

13.31 If you have fitted a tapered head stock bearing and you find that the headlamp brackets are loose, add a large O-ring here. If your bike has fork stanchion covers, fit these now.

13.29 Insert the rubbers in both top and bottom of the headlamp bracket.

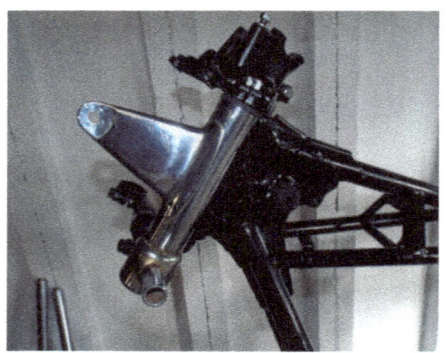

13.30 Insert the headlamp brackets between top and bottom yokes before sliding in the forks.

13.32 Slide the fork stanchion through until it sits flush to the top of the yoke, and so that you can access the top nut easily.

REBUILD

13.33 Check both fork stanchions are of equal height.

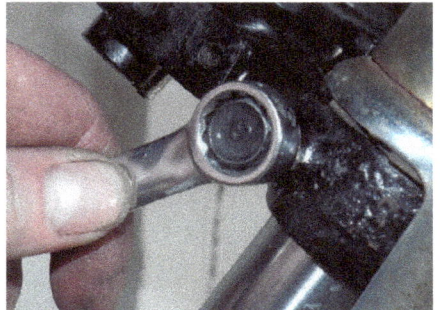

13.34 Tighten both top and bottom bolts.

13.35 Now fit any other rubbers that you have for the frame: these are the fuel tank supporting rubbers.

13.36 Fit the ignition switch now. Some are located by the handlebars, whilst others live on the side of the frame underneath the fuel tank.

13.37 Two bolts hold the complete clock (instrument) assembly in position. Remember to fit the rubbers.

13.38 The clocks are rubber-mounted, and require a good-sized washer on each side to prevent the nut from pulling through.

13.39 Once the forks are in place refit the front wheel by lifting into position, sliding the disk (rotor) into the caliper and bolting on the fork end caps securely.

HOW TO RESTORE HONDA FOURS

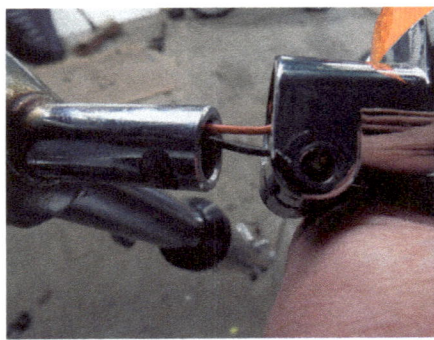

13.40 On this model the indicators are fitted to the headlamp brackets. On others the indicators fit directly to the headlamp bowl. Push the wires through the bracket and into the headlamp bowl ...

13.41 ... and then push the indicators onto the bracket and replace the small nut and bolt.

13.42 Don't forget to fit the cable guides at this stage. Not all cables have them, though there are usually one or two for the speedometer and/or brake hose.

13.43 Fit the hydraulic brakes to the hose joint underneath the bottom yoke. This also houses the front brake light switch on earlier models. Later models have the brake light switch in the brake lever.

The headlamp rubbers should be fitted before fitting the headlamp bowl. The rubbers are important, and prevent the cables wearing through on the edge of the metal headlamp bowl.

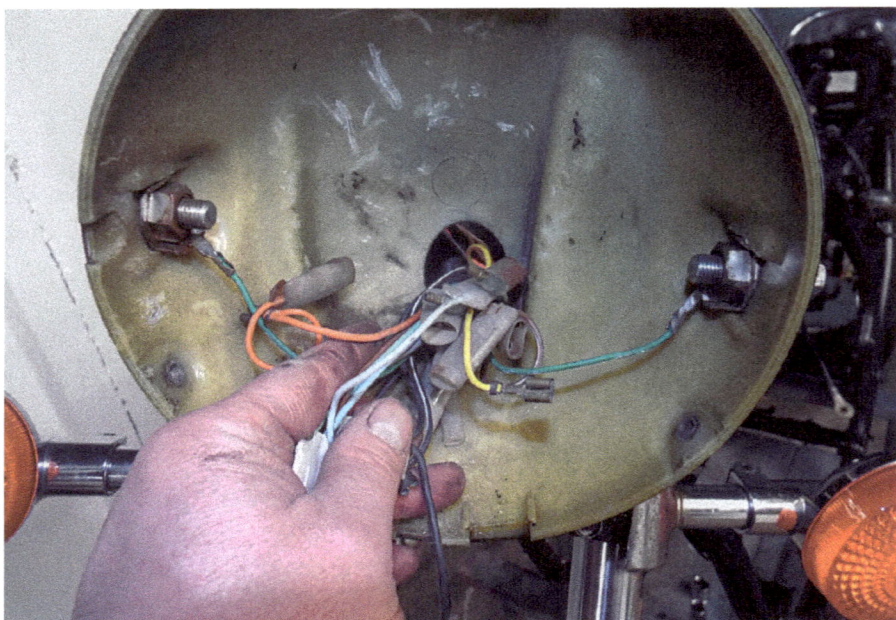

13.44 If you find it difficult to push all of the cables through the headlamp bowl, it may be easier to push some of the loom connectors through the back of the headlamp just before bolting it in. Start with the bigger connectors and work down in size until the last wires are single earth wires. If you push the connectors through randomly it will be difficult to push the big connectors through a big bunch of wires.

REBUILD

13.45 If the seat that holds the inner nut is worn, use two spanners to bolt the headlamp bowl onto the brackets. Pull all the wires through into the headlamp bowl.

FITTING THE REAR WHEEL

Before fitting the rear wheel to the frame, correctly reassemble all main components (front wheel, sprocket carrier, and brake hub). Most SOHC Fours have drum brakes on the back, but yours may be a later model with a disk brake. This will bolt directly to the wheel. Installing the rear wheel and brake calliper on later models is the same as it was with the front wheel and brake calliper described in 13.39.

13.48 The sprocket carrier is then placed into the rubbers of the cush drive. Here, a sprocket drum retainer can also be seen.

13.46 Check the rubber cush drive/shock absorber for wear. If this is damaged, replace it. Fortunately, most are in a reusable condition.

13.47 Check all bolts are tight, and that there's no debris inside.

13.49 Now place the brake hub into the drum.

153

HOW TO RESTORE HONDA FOURS

13.50 Insert the rear wheel spindle to hold all parts in position, making sure that the spacers are in the correct position.

13.51 With the sprocket carrier fitted it should look like this.

13.52 The rear brake lever return spring should be fitted as shown, with the protruding end resting on the back of the swinging arm.

13.53 When refitting the rear brake pivot arm, ensure this is positioned in front of the swinging arm.

13.54 Lift the rear wheel and push the spindle onto the swinging arm.

13.55 Some models have a wear limit sticker on the rear wheel adjuster. Most models have frame markings that can be aligned with the line on the adjuster on both sides to ensure that the rear wheel is straight before the axle nut is tightened.

REBUILD

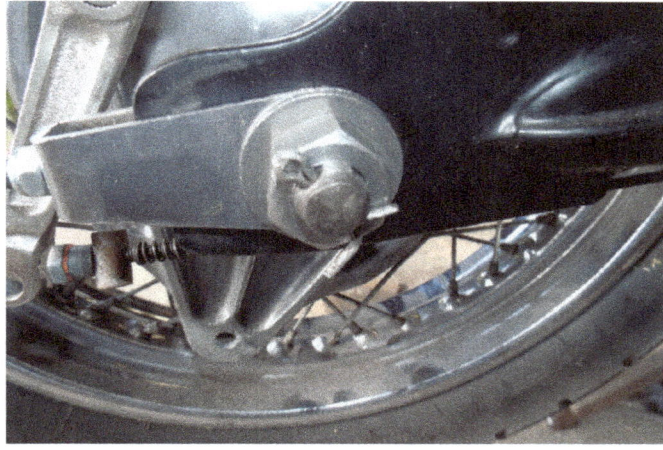

13.56 It's very important to fit a split pin once the nut is in place.

13.59 Insert the brake rod and spring.

13.57 The chain adjuster support should go in now.

13.60 Now screw on the rear brake rod adjuster nut.

13.58 Place the small cable locator in the brake cam lever.

13.61 The rear brake torque arm fits inside the bracket on the underneath of the swinging arm. This bolt must have a split pin fitted.

HOW TO RESTORE HONDA FOURS

13.62 Fit the rear wheel torque arm to the brake hub. Always use a split pin on both ends of the torque arm.

13.63 Adjust rear brake to the manufacturer's recommended setting.

REFITTING THE ENGINE

With both wheels on and the bike on the centre stand (if fitted) we can put the engine in. Ask someone to help you with this, as even the smaller SOHC engines are very heavy.

13.64 This size of engine is most certainly a two-person job to get back in the frame.

13.65 Use a car jack, with a piece of wood on the lifting pad, to take the strain. Then carefully lift the engine into position.

13.66 With the jack supporting the engine, slowly lower it until the engine mounting holes line up correctly. Put all the engine mounting bolts in position and tighten to the specified torque. Remember any engine mounting rubbers and the footrests, too.

REBUILD

13.67 Connect the HT caps to the sparkplugs.

13.70 Replace the throttle cables and, in the case of later models, the choke cable, too.

13.68 Refit the carburettor rubbers. Most are numbered to show correct order (my CB350F didn't have these numbers so it was necessary to mark them when removing). See pictures 13.72/73.

13.71 Reassemble all of the air filter parts, and fit a new filter element. Then refit the complete unit. If your air filter has them, connect any breather pipes.

13.69 When fitting the carburettors, check the worm drive clips are facing in the same direction on each side, and line them up to give a uniform appearance.

13.72 If the air filter or carburettor filter rubbers have gone hard, soaking them in cellulose thinners for an hour will soften them.

HOW TO RESTORE HONDA FOURS

13.73 Soft again, and much easier to put back on.

13.74 If the front chain sprocket was not put on while the engine was on the bench now is the time to fit it.

13.75 Screw in the tachometer cable.

13.76 Refit the rear brake lever and adjust for correct operation.

13.77 Connect the spring to the brake leaver and light switch and adjust properly when the electrics are connected. The rear light should come on before the brakes begin to hold the rear wheel.

REBUILD

13.78 In most cases the chain and sprockets will be worn and in poor condition, necessitating a new set. Try to get the correct sprocket sizes that were fitted originally, as this will ensure that the gearing is as it was designed by Honda.

13.80 Make sure that the engine is in neutral and pull the chain over the top of the sprocket and all the way back until the two ends of the chain meet in the middle.

13.79 Place the chain on the rear sprocket and feed it forward, toward the front sprocket.

13.81 Push the link through the two eyes in the end of the chain, completing the loop.

HOW TO RESTORE HONDA FOURS

13.82 Place the other side of the link on the two link pins and push it back firmly, ensuring that the rear part of the link is pushed all the way through (you should see the slots in the pins at the ends).

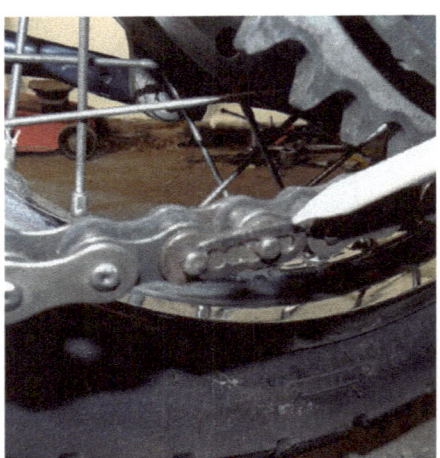

13.83 Slide the split link onto the two slots as shown.

13.84 Making sure that the round end faces the direction of rotation, tightly squeeze the end of the split link and one of the pins until the open end of the split link is forced over the second slot.

13.85 Once the link has been fitted it should look like this. You can see the split end has clipped firmly around the second pin.

13.86 Now adjust the two rear axle bolts evenly until the wheel is straight and the chain has the recommended amount of slackness. Vertical movement of ...

REBUILD

FITTING THE EXHAUST

13.87 ... 15-20mm (½-¾ inch) is recommended.

13.89 Do not over-tighten the nuts: it's common, here, for threads to strip, and for the nuts to come loose after a while, so keep an eye on these and retighten when necessary.

13.88 When fitting the exhaust system always use new exhaust manifold gaskets. Use a little grease on the gasket, as this will prevent it dropping out when positioning the exhaust pipes.

13.90 Fitting the exhaust can be tricky, and you would certainly benefit from having an assistant. Once the front of the exhaust is in position, fit the rear bracket to the frame using the footpeg bolt, then, when everything's in place, fully tighten the manifold and rear bracket nuts.

HOW TO RESTORE HONDA FOURS

13.91 Now replace the seat and slide in the two seat pins.

13.93 Refit the fuel tank and connect the fuel line to the carburettors.

13.92 With the seat on, check that it lifts and closes properly, and that the seat catch and lock line up.

13.94 Replace the side panels.

REBUILD

13.95 Now all the major parts are refitted to your bike you have completed your restoration, with only minor adjustments remaining. I hope you are happy with the end result and enjoy riding it.

Chapter 14
Final details

By now you should have what looks like a very presentable motorcycle. It may not be perfect: as previously noted, some spare parts might prove difficult to source, necessitating continued use of a part you would really rather have changed. Nevertheless, you're almost there and ready to set up your bike.

With all of the main components in place, your motorcycle is almost ready to ride. A few settings and adjustments should be carried out at this stage, as detailed in the workshop manual. Many are common to most motorcycles, however, and these are the ones I go through in this chapter. First, though, check that all nuts, bolts and screws are tight, as it's easy to miss one or two.

CABLES

The first point to mention about cables – be they clutch or brake – is that the correct versions for your motorcycle should be used. Pattern parts are fine, but cables from another make or model will not do. Cable length, types of nipple and adjusters can be quite different from one motorcycle to another.

All of the cables on your motorcycle will have adjusters, and some have one at each end of the cable. These are intended to help set the correct amount of tension or slack in the cable.

14.1 Looking first at the clutch cable, a good starting point is to aim for around 3-4mm (⅛ inch) of slack at the clutch lever. This ensures that the clutch is fully engaged and will not slip when riding. If the cable is too tight, the clutch will be slightly disengaged, causing the clutch to slip and wear early. Use the adjuster at the clutch lever end of the cable to set the slack, but never unscrew it so much that it is on the limit of the thread.

14.2 If there is not enough adjustment on the cable at the clutch lever end, you can also make adjustment to this end. Only when you ride your motorcycle will you know if the clutch is adjusted properly, but if the clutch plates are in good condition and there's 3-4mm (⅛ inch) of slack at the clutch lever, I would say the clutch is adjusted correctly and should work fine.

FINAL DETAILS

14.3 Now onto the brakes. The hydraulic disk front brake normally needs no adjustment at the lever, although some models do have a brake lever adjuster bolt by which to set lever travel. Adjustment is also carried out at the brake calliper to take up any wear in the front disk pads, and not to adjust the position of the brake lever.

The rear brake on models with a drum brake are adjusted by loosening the locknut on the brake rod and turning the adjuster until the brake is set correctly. On all models there's also a rear brake lever travel adjuster, which should be set to give 25mm (1 inch) of travel.

THROTTLE CABLE

The throttle cable should be free moving, and snap back under spring pressure when released after opening to full throttle position. The cable should have 1mm of free play at the carburettor end. If the cable has been routed correctly, this amount should not alter when the handlebars are turned full lock in both directions.

14.4 The cable adjusters should be locked with the locking nuts when the desired setting is achieved.

14.5 This adjuster is used to set the correct cable length. Adjust both the push and pull cable until happy with the throttle action, and so that the engine will speed up with a slight opening of the throttle. Only use the idle adjuster to adjust the engine tickover speed.

BRAKE LIGHTS

14.6 It is often the case that the rear brake light spring requires shortening to allow proper adjustment of the brake light. To do this, simply snip off the required amount, and bend the end to the original shape.

HOW TO RESTORE HONDA FOURS

MIRRORS
Correctly setting the mirrors is a simple but important procedure. Some motorcycles have only one mirror, though most have one on each side of the handlebars.

14.7 Sitting on the motorcycle whilst off the stands, set the mirrors so that you cannot see your own reflection. This may not be 100 per cent possible but you need to see as much as possible of the road and traffic behind. Try to set them to view slightly different distances behind you.

TYRE PRESSURE AND TREAD
Check tyre pressures match those set by Honda, and that the tyres are not worn or damaged.

SPLIT PINS
Re-check that all castle nuts have split pins in, and that the split pin has been bent open.

LIGHTS
Check that all of the lights are working and that the headlight beam is set to the correct angle. Each country will have different height requirements, check your local regulations, and adjust accordingly.

14.8 The headlight adjustment screws are located on the headlamp bowl, allowing for easy adjustment.

FIRST START UP
Before you start your motorcycle, some essential checks are required –
• Check the oil is to the correct level
• Put in fresh fuel
• Did you fit new sparkplugs? If not, are the old ones clean and showing a spark?
• Is the battery topped up with de-ionized water (if appropriate) and fully charged?

14.9 Turn on the ignition.

14.11 Set the choke to the 'on' position.

166

FINAL DETAILS

14.11 Make sure the engine kill switch is in the 'run' position, and turn the fuel tap to the 'on' position. Check that the bike is not in gear (pull in the clutch on some models) and press the starter. Slightly open the throttle each time you to this. It may take a few attempts, especially if the engine has been rebuilt, but after 2-3 tries it should fire. Once it fires and begins to run, let it warm a little before opening the throttle any more (if you open the throttle too early the engine will flood and will be more difficult to start the next time).

maintenance checks in your workshop manual recommended by the manufacturer, many of which are also set out here.
- Check engine oil level
- Check brake fluid level
- Check front and rear brakes are correctly adjusted
- Check chain tension
- Lubricate the chain
- Check that all lights and indicators work correctly
- Check there is enough fuel for your ride
- Check clutch lever play
- Check for leaks

After it has run on tickover for a minute or two, slowly open the throttle to increase the revs: this will warm the engine quicker and get it up to running temperature.

Does it sound okay? Keep an eye out for leaks, especially petrol leaks. The most common leak at this stage is from the carburettors overflowing because the valve in the float bowl has not been seated properly, or has a tiny piece of dirt preventing it from closing. Try gently tapping the float bowl with a piece of wood: this often resolves it and stops the leak.

Does the engine settle to a nice tickover if you open the throttle and then close it again? It often takes several attempts at setting the carburettors before the engine runs evenly and at the right rpm.

If the engine doesn't misfire, ticks over nicely, and will rev cleanly, it sounds as though you've done a good job of setting up the engine: well done!

THE FIRST RIDE

If the bike is running well, you'll be keen to take it out. Check you have all of the necessary legal requirements (insurance, tax, etc) in place before setting off. Go through all the basic

Don't go too far on your first run. There are usually teething troubles after a rebuild, and you don't want to break down miles away from home.

A couple of laps around the block are enough, and then come back and check that everything is okay. Gradually, you can increase ride range as you become confident that your newly rebuilt bike is not going to break down on you.

If the engine has been rebuilt, remember to run it in as recommended by the manufacturer. Everything will be new and tight, and will require some gentle mileage before using the full rev range.

Usually after a short running-in period the cylinder head bolts and exhaust bolts need to be torqued again. Once done, keep an eye on fluid levels, and that's it!

Chapter 15
Safe riding

It is a chilling fact that motorcyclists make up less than 1 per cent of all traffic, yet bike riders account for 19 per cent of all road user deaths on Britain's roads (Think! 2014), and this sad statistic is repeated in many countries across the world. Following some basic guidance, and attending a rider training course will increase your chances of staying safe on the road.

Many motorcycle restorations involve bikes that individuals had in their youth, for one reason or another (better jobs, girlfriends, marriage and kids) having given up motorcycling subsequently but never losing their love for it, nostalgically recalling long hot summers and empty roads. Things have changed a lot since then, of course, and much more care is needed out on the roads. Whether a seasoned rider, new to motorcycling, or returning after a long absence, make safety your priority.

When I first had motorcycles there were far fewer cars on the road than there are now. I remember playing football in the road as a teenager, when my friends and I had to get out of the way of the odd car or two that passed. You could never play football in that same road now, and even in a small village setting there's usually a constant stream of traffic.

If returning to riding a bike, make your first few rides at quiet times, maybe going out earlier or later in the day, or on Sundays.

THE COUNTRY ROAD STORY

Returning to riding again was an eye-opener for me. I thought I knew how to ride: I knew I *used* to know how to ride, but it soon became obvious that I had almost to learn again how to ride. After a short ride I found I was taking a wider than necessary line through corners, as bends seemed to get tighter and tighter, and I was going much further out than I was comfortable with, almost on the opposite side of the road. My country road run was suddenly not so appealing, with a tractor heading in my direction and me almost in his lane. I pulled it back in time but it certainly gave me a wake-up call.

I had remembered the long rides I used to take with my pals, but forgotten slippery manhole covers, white lines, cat's eyes and potholes. I realised on this first short journey that I really did need to take things easy and get used to riding again; only then would I be able to enjoy my motorcycling the way I remembered it.

Consider joining a club, all of which welcome new members, and have regular ride-outs. Apart from anything else, a group of motorcyclists is much more visible on the road than a lone rider. Remember the old saying: safety in numbers.

15.1 Clubs often carry out important voluntary work. These guys deliver emergency blood supplies for local hospitals.

SAFE RIDING

15.2 This group has medically trained volunteers in rural areas who can attend the scene of an accident and offer initial treatment before the ambulance arrives.

Wear the appropriate clothing and buy the best you can afford. Make sure you have a good pair of motorcycle boots, a good jacket, trousers, gloves, and crash helmet.

Be seen: wear a high visibility vest or jacket, and keep the headlamp on at all the times, day and night.

Keep a simple, all-weather kit under your seat. Even in the summer you can get caught out and, once you're wet, the rest of the ride will be miserable.

Learn to ride defensively, expect every car, van, lorry – and even another motorcycle – to pull out in front of you at junctions. Be ready with your brakes and drive carefully past junctions.

Keep a safe distance between you and the vehicle in front; if the vehicle behind is a little too close, make some space for yourself by pulling ahead if you can do so without exceeding the speed limit, or slow down and allow the vehicle to pass.

When filtering between traffic watch out for other vehicles changing lanes, which is most likely to happen when there's a junction ahead. I was slowly filtering between traffic on an old Honda Goldwing once, when a car driver noticed that his door wasn't closed properly. Just as I approached he opened the door quickly and slammed it shut, and I narrowly missed crashing into it.

OVERTAKING

Some of the following points are obvious but well worth mentioning.

Do not overtake at junctions, pedestrian crossings, hills or bends. The classic accident is the rider who is overtaking a car that has failed to indicate, but nevertheless turns just as the motorcycle pulls alongside. There will be only one winner here, so beware.

15.3 This thin line of spilt diesel spells danger for a motorcyclist.

BAD ROAD CONDITIONS

It's often claimed that motorcyclists who have had off-road riding experience – such as motocross or trials riding – are safer riders than those who have not, and a reason cited for this is that the riding surface is changing all the time, from muddy soil to wet slopes and sand or slippery rocks. The rider learns to change their riding style to suit the conditions, and learns to react quickly: a useful skill that all riders would do well to develop. Look ahead for signs of potential hazards.

Keep a check on road surface conditions. A diesel spill – a shiny wet line on a dry road or the shimmering colours of the rainbow on wet ones – is very common on corners and roundabouts ... but very dangerous for a motorcyclist. Look ahead for mud and leaves on the road, especially in the wet, and on rural roads grain spills, which are like marbles to a motorcyclist.

A shower after a long, dry spell means the road surface will be more slippery than normal because it has

15.4 A rain shower after a dry spell makes for a slippery road surface.

15.5 Regularly check your tyres for sufficient tread and correct pressure to avoid mishaps on wet and/or slippery roads.

rubber on the surface caused by traffic. Rain sits on the rubber and makes a very slippery surface.

TRAINING
Almost all countries have safety organisations that offer training and advice for motorcyclists, and these are well worth becoming involved with. In the UK there is The Bikesafe scheme, which is run by the police, and the Advanced Motorcyclist's scheme, run by the Institute of Advanced Motorists, whilst the USA has courses run by The Motorcycling Safety Foundation.

Enjoy your riding – and be safe!

15.6 Road safety is in everyone's interest, and is promoted at most motorcycle events.

More motorcycle titles from Veloce Publishing

Ducati Bevel Twins

Ducati's classic 750, 860, 900 and Mille bevel-drive twins from 1971-1986 are now amongst the most collectable bikes in the world. This book serves as a definitive guide to authenticity, and gives hands-on restoration tips and guidance.

ISBN: 978-1-787111-81-3
Paperback • 27x20.7cm • 288 pages

Italian Custom Motorcycles

Many books have been published about Italian motorcycles, but none has focused exclusively on the Italian motorcycle-based chopper, bobber, trike, and quad custom bike scene ... until now. A book to inspire and entertain.

ISBN: 978-1-845843-94-6
Hardback • 25x25cm • 128 pages

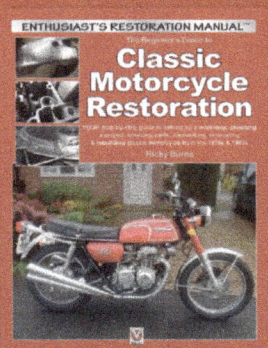

Classic Motorcycle Restoration

In this book, seasoned motorcycle restorer Ricky Burns takes you through each of the stages of real-life restorations. Aimed at enthusiasts of all abilities, from the total beginner to those with experience already, the reader is shown each stage and process in step-by-step detail, along with the techniques, tricks and tips used by experts. From choosing a project, setting up a workshop, and preparing a motorcycle, to sourcing parts, dismantling, restoring and renovating, this book is the perfect guide for the classic motorcycle restorer.

ISBN: 978-1-845846-44-2
Paperback • 27x20.7cm • 144 pages

Tales of Triumph Motorcycles

Hughie worked at Triumph from 1954 until its closure in 1974. Here's the story of his life in the famous Meriden factory; of many adventures with Triumph motorcycles & Triumph people. Records the fascinating history of a great marque.

ISBN: 978-1-787115-49-1
Paperback • 25x20.7cm • 144 pages

The Café Racer Phenomenon

The Café Racer is one of the most enduring styles of motorcycle ever created, encapsulating the rebellious spirit of the 50s. Featuring a huge, global Café Racer directory alongside a unique mix of personal memories, previously unseen photos, iconic machines and chassis builders in profile, this book is a must for any 'ton-up' rider.

ISBN: 978-1-845842-64-2
Paperback • 19x20.5cm • 96 pages

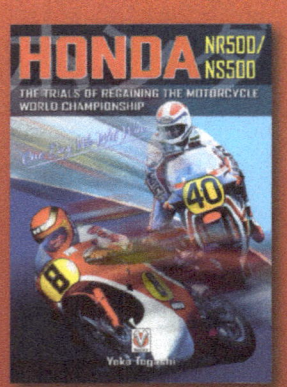

Honda NR500/NS500

Honda's 4-stroke heritage allowed world motor cycle racing and sales domination. However, in the 1970s two strokes dominated racing, damaging 4-stroke sales. A winning 4-stroke Honda GP racer was needed, but it was a glorious failure. Finally, Honda went 2-stroke; the resulting NS500 Honda eventually met success in 1983. This is the first in house analysis of the amazing NR500 Grand Prix Honda.

ISBN: 978-1-787115-77-4
Hardback • 14.8x21cm • 192 pages

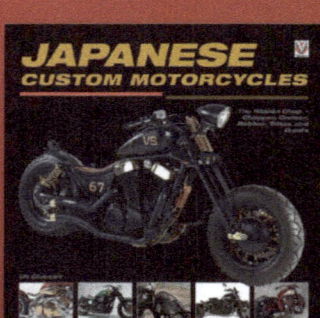

Japanese Custom Motorcycles

The first book to solely cover the evolution of the Japanese cruiser into metric custom, Japanese Custom Motorcycles is an insight into the growing trend of customising metric bikes into chopper, bobber et al, et al – be they high-end bikes, garage built beauties, or more recent Japanese cruisers. Superbly illustrated with examples from all over the world, and featuring owner's stories and technical descriptions, this book is guaranteed to interest metric bike fans and members of the custom scene alike – see the 'custom' side of Japanese motorcycles.

ISBN: 978-1-845845-30-8
Hardback • 25x25cm • 128 pages

The Essential Buyer's Guides

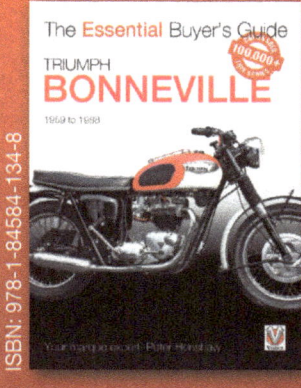
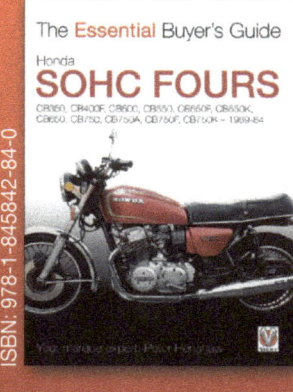
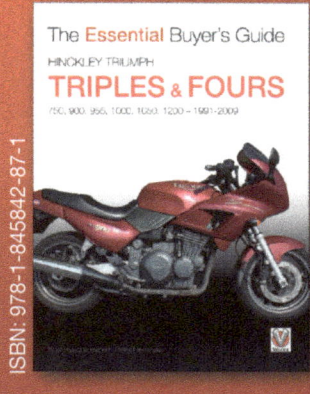
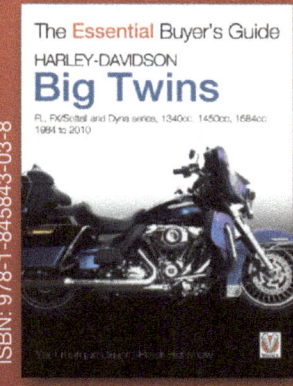

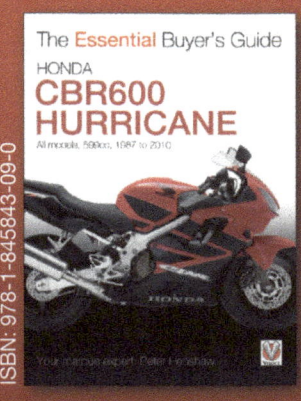
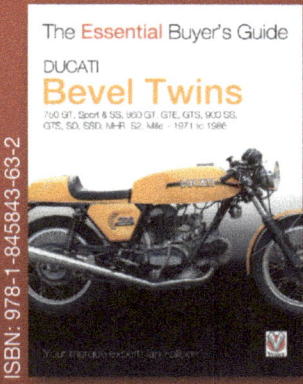

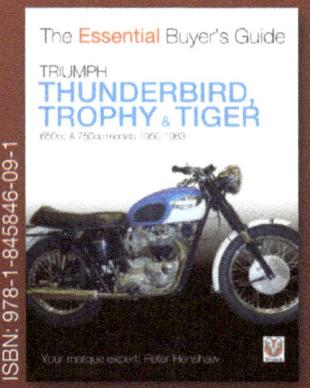

For more info on Veloce titles, visit our website at www.veloce.co.uk   email: info@veloce.co.uk   Tel: +44(0)1305 260068

eBooks from Veloce Publishing

From technical manuals, to photo books, to autobiographies, Veloce's range of eBooks gives you the same high-quality content, but in a digital format tailored to your favourite e-reader. Whether it's a technical manual, an autobiography, or a factual account of motorsport history, Veloce's ever expanding eBook range offers something for everyone.

See our website for information on our full range of eBook titles.

www.veloce.co.uk

For news, competitions and information **tweet/like/subscribe** to Veloce's social networks

 /VelocePublishing   /VelocePublishing   @velocebooks

Index

Air filter	18, 157	Cylinder head	42, 45, 67, 69	Light, rear	147
Alternator	105			Lock, seat	147
Assembly grease	56	Decals	112, 113		
Auto jumble	13, 14	Decarbonisation	4, 7	Mirrors	166
		Duck	84	Mudguard	20, 146, 147
Battery	15, 101				
Bearings, head stock	24, 25, 149	Engine	19, 37, 156	Oil pump	49, 51, 59
Big end bearing	55	Exhaust	19, 98	Oil tank	148
Brake				Overtaking	169, 170
Adjustment	164, 165	Filler	110		
Caliper	72, 75	Filter, air	18, 157	Paint	27, 28
Disk	76, 80	Filter, oil	70	Paint stripping	109
Drum	78, 79	Fork oil	139	Piston and rings	48, 65
Hose	72, 75, 76	Fork seals	142	Polishing	31, 33, 82
Master cylinder	76, 77	Forks	10, 138-143	Preparation	109-111
Piston	78	Frame	26-28, 144	Primary chain	52
Shoes	79, 80	Fuel tank	9, 17, 87, 162	Primer	110
		Fuel tap	15, 87, 89		
Cabinet blaster	34	Fuse	103	Rectifier	105
Cam chain	58, 67, 68			Road conditions	169, 170
Cam chain tensioner	42, 69	Gaskets	55, 66	Rubbers	148, 151, 157
Camshaft	42, 43	Gear shaft	38		
Carburettor rubbers	90	Gears	52, 53, 57	Seals	55, 57, 66, 67
Carburettor	18, 91, 92, 93, 94, 95, 96, 97, 157			Seat	10, 17, 128-137, 162
		Headlamp	20, 22	Cover	134
Chain	18, 159-161	HT cap	104	Trim	135
Clocks	123-127			Shock absorber	21, 145
Clutch	38, 40, 61, 62, 63	Ignition, points	64, 103	Side panels	18, 162
Adjustment	164	Indicators	20, 152	Solenoid	105
Plates	39, 40	Inner tube	83	Sparkplug	15, 104
Coil	104, 147	Internet	12	Spraying	27, 28, 109, 110, 111
Crankshaft	54, 56			Sprockets	61, 154, 158, 159
Cush drive	82, 153	Jets, carburettor	94, 95	Stands	25, 145

175

HOW TO RESTORE HONDA FOURS

Starter motor	70, 106, 107	Tappets	42, 69
Stripes	112-117	Torque arm	21, 155
Swinging arm	25, 145	Tyres	83, 84
Swinging arm bushes	26, 145		
Switchgear	23, 118-122	Ultra sonic cleaner	30, 89
Tachometer cable	158	Valves	42, 45, 46

Voltage regulator	105
Wheels	21, 22, 81, 83
Wiring	17, 102, 147

www.ingramcontent.com/pod-product-compliance
Lightning Source LLC
Chambersburg PA
CBHW040739300426
44111CB00026B/2984